MW01234579

2005

Personal Prayer Journal

Devote yourselves to prayer,
being watchful and thankful.

Colossians 4:2

WORLD WIDE PUBLICATIONS
Charlotte, North Carolina 28266

2005 Personal Prayer Journal

Deluxe Illustrated Cover Edition
© 2004 World Wide Publications

ISBN: 0-89066-341-6
Printed in Canada

Contents

The Importance of Prayer

Prayer is our most important work as Christians. It is a journey filled with the satisfaction of helping the helpless, and of seeing the purposes of God fulfilled and the strategies of Satan thwarted. In the unseen arena of prayer the real work of God is forged. We often see the results in the visible world, but God is moving behind the scenes, acting in response to those who labor daily in prayer.

Exodus 17 illustrates this principle vividly. As the Israelite army fought the Amalekites on the plain of Rephidim, Moses stood on a hill overlooking the battle. Whenever he held up the staff of God, Israel prevailed. But when he lowered the staff, the Amalekites gained the advantage. A clear principle of prayer emerges from this account: God acts in response to the prayers of His intercessors, supernaturally enabling those He has called to accomplish the assigned task. Moses' part in the victory, though probably unseen and unnoticed by those in the fight, was vital.

Our role in the work of God throughout the world may be unnoticed, unseen, unappreciated. But, like Moses, God calls us to "hold up the staff of God"—to pray. In fact, God is looking "for a man among them who would build up the wall and stand before me in the gap on behalf of the land so I would not have to destroy it, but I found none" (Ezekiel 22:30). We need to take our part in the plan and program of God seriously, developing the attitude that Samuel had toward Israel when he said, "As for me, far be it from me that I should sin against the LORD by failing to pray for you" (1 Samuel 12:23).

Prayer is work. Prayer is hard work. But prayer is a holy work as well—vital and indispensable. God has a more difficult time finding people for *prayer* than He does for any other assignment.

THE PERSONAL PRAYER JOURNAL IS DESIGNED

1. To provide practical insights from God's Word on prayer.

2. To provide a suggested plan for a prayer ministry that is manageable, measurable, and useful.

3. To provide the means of making prayer ministry a reality.

> In order to make a tool like the *Personal Prayer Journal* work, we need the determination to be faithful to the commitment.

1. Our primary responsibility is to be faithful to pray. The results of our prayers are God's responsibility.

2. We need to be realistic in our prayer ministry. Faithfulness to a short, daily prayer time is more desirable than occasional faithfulness to an unrealistic larger time commitment.

3. We should make daily entries of significant prayer items in the space provided on the calendar pages. These will become a source of tremendous encouragement and motivation as we look back at the written record of how God answered specific prayers.

4. The *Personal Prayer Journal* is designed for only one aspect of our spiritual life—prayer. We must not neglect regular reading and meditation in God's Word.

Principles of Prayer

As we begin to develop a personal prayer strategy, we need to examine some principles of prayer from God's Word. Three vital aspects of prayer are Attitudes in Prayer, Obstacles to Prayer, and Answers to Prayer.

ATTITUDES IN PRAYER

Prayer is conversation with God. But when we talk with God it is not just like any other conversation. There are several qualities that should mark our attitudes as we converse with our Creator:

Awe. When John the apostle saw the glorified Christ, he "fell at his feet as though dead" (Revelation 1:17). When the prophet Isaiah had his vision of the throne room of God, he exclaimed, "Woe to me! . . . I am ruined! For I am a man of unclean lips, and I live among a people of unclean lips, and my eyes have seen the King, the Lord Almighty" (Isaiah 6:5).

Yet, as A. W. Tozer has said,

> We go to God as we send a boy to a grocery store with a long written list, "God, give me this," and our gracious God often gives us what we want. But I think God is disappointed because we make Him no more than a source of what we want.

Awe simply means being constantly amazed at who God is and that He would even allow us to address Him as "Father."

Helplessness. We must be genuinely convinced of our own inability to accomplish the thing for which we are praying to God. O. Hallesby, in his classic book, *Prayer,* highlights this truth when he says:

> Be not anxious because of your helplessness. Above all, do not let it prevent you from praying. Helplessness is the real secret and the impelling power of prayer. You should therefore rather try to thank God for the feeling of helplessness which He has

given you. It is one of the greatest gifts which God can impart to us. For it is only when we are helpless that we open our hearts to Jesus and let Him help us in our distress, according to His grace and mercy.

The apostle Paul similarly speaks of our total inability to accomplish anything on our own in the spiritual realm. He confesses, "You see, at just the right time, when we were still powerless, Christ died for the ungodly" (Romans 5:6). And again in Romans 8:26 he says, "The Spirit helps us in our weakness. We do not know what we ought to pray for."

The proper starting place in prayer, then, is an awe of God, which in turn makes us see our own helplessness. It is the realization that we are totally powerless within ourselves to make our prayers happen. Our helplessness induces prayer.

Faith. But it takes more than helplessness. It is faith that shapes the cries of our hearts into genuine prayer. Hallesby points out that

Without faith there can be no prayer, no matter how great our helplessness may be. Helplessness united with faith produces prayer. Without faith our helplessness would only be a vain cry of distress in the night.

The writer of Hebrews agrees:

And without faith it is impossible to please God, because anyone who comes to him must believe that he exists and that he rewards those who earnestly seek him (11:6).

But faith is often the very thing we feel that we lack in our prayer life. Perhaps we do not understand that in the very act of praying we are demonstrating faith. By going to God, we exercise genuine faith. It may be a young faith, but it *is* faith! We have "faith enough" when we turn to Jesus in our helplessness. The *results* of prayer are the concern of God. *Our* concern is to come to Him in prayer with the awareness that we are helpless in ourselves.

Confidence. The essence of faith is our confidence in God's ability to do what He has promised. Abraham stands as our clearest illustration of confident faith:

> *Yet he did not waver through unbelief regarding the promise of God, but was strengthened in his faith and gave glory to God, being fully persuaded that God had power to do what he had promised (Romans 4:20–21).*

Too often we unconsciously shift our faith from confidence in God's ability to do what He has promised, to confidence in our ability to believe He will do a certain thing. In other words, we put our confidence in our faith rather than in God! Jesus makes it clear that the *size* of our faith is not what matters when He says, "I tell you the truth, if you have faith as small as a mustard seed, you can say to this mountain, 'Move from here to there' and it will move. Nothing will be impossible for you" (Matthew 17:20). It is the *object* of our faith—God—that is the basis of our confidence in prayer.

Persistence. In Matthew 7:7 Jesus says, "Ask and it will be given to you; seek and you will find; knock and the door will be opened to you." This verse translated literally says, "Ask and keep on asking . . . seek and keep on seeking . . . knock and keep on knocking." It shows us the importance of persistent prayer, of continuing to bring our prayers to God. Even Jesus, on the night of His betrayal, brought His anguished plea to the Father three times before relenting.

OBSTACLES TO PRAYER

Even the most mature Christians will sometimes feel that their prayers are not getting "beyond the ceiling." There are several things that can seriously hinder our prayer life:

Unconfessed Sin. David confessed, "If I had cherished sin in my heart, the Lord would not have listened" (Psalm 66:18). Isaiah tells us, "Surely the arm of the LORD is not too short to save, nor his ear too dull to hear. But your iniquities have separated you from your God; your sins have hidden his face from you, so that he will not hear" (Isaiah 59:1–2).

Sin renders our prayers useless because it alienates us from the object of our prayers—God. When we are out of fellowship with God due to unconfessed sin in our lives, our prayers are powerless monologues. We need to confess our sins of anger, lust, envy, gossip, or whatever else that has become a barrier between us and our Father. The basis of our access in prayer is fellowship with God.

Broken Fellowship with Others. Too often, "fellowship" is mistakenly understood to be an activity, when in fact it is a condition. Fellowship is not so much something we do as something we are either in or out of. The apostle John illuminates this for us:

> If we claim to have fellowship with him yet walk in the darkness, we lie and do not live by the truth. But if we walk in the light, as he is in the light, we have fellowship with one another, and the blood of Jesus, his Son, purifies us from all sin (1 John 1:6–7).

It is clear from this passage that our relationship with God is inseparably linked to our relationship with other believers. We cannot go to God in prayer when we are out of fellowship with one of His other children. Jesus emphasized this truth to His disciples in the Sermon on the Mount when He said:

> Therefore, if you are offering your gift at the altar and there remember that your brother has something against you, leave your gift there in front of the altar. First go and be reconciled to your brother; then come and offer your gift (Matthew 5:23–24).

Restitution of broken relationships is a prerequisite to effective prayer. This principle applies to relationships both inside and outside the church; it is especially relevant within the home. The apostle Peter said that conflict between spouses will "hinder" their prayers (1 Peter 3:7).

We can safely say in the light of these Scriptures that if we are not on speaking terms with God's people, we are not on speaking terms with God either. As with unconfessed sin in general, we should make immediate efforts to restore any broken relationship before we resume the ministry of intercession. If restoration is not possible immediately, we need to confess this broken fellowship to

God and make a commitment to *Him* to deal with it as soon as possible.

Wrong Motives. A final obstacle to prayer has to do with the intention of our hearts. James warns us,

> *When you ask, you do not receive, because you ask with wrong motives, that you may spend what you get on your pleasures (James 4:3).*

If we pray for things that will feed that part of us known as our "sinful nature" (Romans 7:18), we cannot expect those prayers to reach the heart of God. Why not? Because God's goal for each one of us is to transform us into the likeness of His Son, Jesus Christ (Romans 8:29). God is not pleased to hear prayer that is contrary to His plans and purposes for our lives. But John assures us that we will be heard when we pray according to His will (1 John 5:14–15).

Our motives, the driving force behind our requests, are crucial factors that can limit the effectiveness of prayer.

ANSWERS TO PRAYER

God has promised to answer our prayers. Yet we need to understand the various forms an answer to prayer can assume. God's answers may sometimes be either a simple "yes" or "no." At other times, the answer may be more complex. The following are four possible ways that God may answer our prayers:

Request Granted. God's Word contains a multitude of promises that we will receive what we ask God for. This is especially true if we pray according to God's specific will for our lives—those things that He wants for us (1 John 5:14–15). Sometimes we pray specifically and God answers specifically. This is a marvelous experience, one that easily fosters courage and motivation for further prayer.

Request Granted, But Not Yet. Isaiah 55:8–9 instructs us that God's thoughts and methods are "higher" than ours—"as the heavens are higher than the earth." Sometimes God's timetable is different from ours! God's answer to our prayers in this case is indeed yes, but we must yield to His schedule. This is an answer, and it is an affirmative answer, but we can easily miss seeing the answer, or believe that God hasn't heard us, simply because the answer hasn't arrived on time. Patience and persistence in prayer are sometimes needed to ensure that we keep looking for God's answer.

Request Granted, But Look Elsewhere. At Jesus' final meal with His disciples, the night of His betrayal, He began to wash their feet (John 13:1–10). Peter was quite offended and when he tried to stop our Lord, Jesus told him that his perspective was wrong (vv. 6–7). Peter was looking so hard for what he expected to see (a conquering Messiah), that he failed to see what was there (a servant Messiah). There are times in prayer when we make a request, fully convinced of what form the answer will take. If God then answers in an unexpected fashion, we may fail to see the answer. We, like Peter, have our minds so made up about what should happen, we fail to see what is actually happening. We need to guard ourselves from unconsciously dictating how God will answer. We must give Him the liberty to be God!

Request Denied. In our relationship with God, sometimes a gradual but serious shift occurs in our own minds regarding who serves whom. Christians can easily forget that God is not a magic genie who jumps at every command. God is God. He is always at liberty to say no to our requests—not capriciously or maliciously, of course, for that would be a denial of His character. But He is still Lord of all. Times will come in our lives when God will deliberately withhold granting requests because of their ultimate effect on our lives or the lives of others. Perhaps the development of certain character qualities in our lives is more vital than the request sought. Withholding answers to prayer must always be understood as His ultimate *protection,* never as *punishment.* Our responsibility during these times of painful denial is to trust in what we know of God's love for us.

The Practice of Prayer

Without this final section, all that has been previously said is merely lifeless information. Talking about prayer is not prayer. To pray effectively, we need to know when, with whom, how, and what to pray.

WHEN TO PRAY

David prayed faithfully in the morning, evening, and often at noon (Psalm 5:3 and 55:17). Our Lord also spent times in prayer during early morning hours and late at night (Mark 1:35 and 6:46 ff.). Much can be said for "opening and closing" each day in communion with God. Often these times provide the most privacy and greatest freedom to be reflective and quiet.

Abraham's chief servant, sent by his master to secure a bride for Isaac, communed with God in the midst of a busy schedule, surrounded by strangers (Genesis 24:11–14). He prayed quietly in his heart (v. 45) in the midst of his work. It is acceptable and advisable to pray throughout the day as well as in the morning and evening. We need not be in the privacy of our homes to seek the face of God. Often, the Lord will bring to mind a person or an issue at the "oddest time." We need to seize these moments and use them to offer short, specific prayers back to God. Learning to respond to the unexpected promptings of the Holy Spirit is vital to a vibrant prayer life.

It is good to have a set time of daily prayer, but it is also important to seize the "eternal moments" that God gives throughout each day.

WITH WHOM TO PRAY

Jesus exhorts us to shun praying in public in order to impress others, and encourages us to pray "in secret" (Matthew 6:5–6). Private prayer will undoubtedly occupy the largest portion of our total prayer life. During these moments of solitude we can unveil our hearts before Him who sees us as we are and yet loves us with an everlasting love. During these private hours we can intercede for the world that exists outside our private place. Here we can plead, weep, or rejoice over issues that matter little to anyone but us and God. Private prayer should be a priority.

But Jesus also speaks of praying with "two or three" (Matthew 18:19–20). The early Christians prayed together often (Acts 4:23–24; 12:12). A sweetness of fellowship and a sense of strength come when God's people go to Him together in prayer.

God's Word holds before us models of private and corporate prayer; both are vital and should have a place in our prayer life.

HOW TO PRAY

It is more important *that* we pray than *how* we pray. Those who pray best are those who pray most. Yet, for some, a very broad format, a sort of "skeleton" model onto which personal detail can be added, is helpful.

A model for how to pray is captured in the acrostic ACTS. Each letter stands for a specific aspect of prayer, arranged in a very natural order:

A—Adoration (worship)

C—Confession (of specific sins)

T—Thanksgiving (gratitude)

S—Supplication (specific requests)

Adoration. Worship begins and ends with who God is. Beginning our prayer time with adoration immediately places us in the position of a creature in the presence of its Creator. Adoration is simply acknowledging to God what He has revealed about Himself. One helpful way to cultivate an attitude of adoration is to take actual phrases from Scripture and "pray them back" to God, using them as springboards of thought on who God is and what He is like. Some of the many appropriate passages for this purpose are Job 38; 1 Chronicles 29:10–13; Psalm 19:1–2; Psalm 84; Psalm 95:1–7; and many other psalms.

Not only is this the proper starting place for prayer, it is a crucial driving force in our entire Christian life. As we worship, we must be sure that the One we worship is indeed the living God.

Confession. The closer we draw to God Himself, the more we sense our own sinfulness. Again like Isaiah, a glimpse of God's glory will cause us to exclaim, "Woe to me" (Isaiah 6:5), as we realize how far we fall short of His glory.

The natural consequence of genuine adoration is sincere confession. It is reasonable that as we worship God, the awareness of our personal sin becomes greater.

Confession is the second step in prayer: agreeing with God that specific conduct and attitudes in our lives are wrong. We should name the sin and ask God to forgive us. During this period of confession, we may also ask God to make us aware of other sins in our life that we are unaware of or have neglected to deal with.

Thanksgiving. Our immediate response after confession is thanksgiving. David said, "Blessed is he whose transgressions are forgiven" (Psalm 32:1). We can certainly thank God for forgiving us of the sins we have just confessed. But gratitude to God should encompass more than forgiveness. Paul told the Colossians,

And whatever you do, whether in word or deed, do it all in the name of the Lord Jesus, giving thanks to God the Father through him (Colossians 3:17).

Thanksgiving causes us to acknowledge God's existence, His love, and His care. It reminds us of His goodness. In short, thanksgiving forces us to keep God in our thoughts.

We should thank God for all the blessings we can see in our lives—health, friends, guidance, and answered prayer. But we should also verbally thank Him for all that is ours that we can't see, such as our adoption as His children, our inheritance in heaven, the ministry of angels in our lives, the new body that will be ours for eternity, and the permanent gift of the Holy Spirit.

By giving thanks, which is simply expressing gratitude for what we have, we prevent our focus from shifting to what we *don't* have. Satan loves to distract God's children from thanksgiving, because he can accomplish much in a heart that is ungrateful. Thanksgiving is a powerful weapon against Satan's tactics.

Supplication. The last step in the ACTS model is supplication—bringing our requests to God. If we are faithful in the first three steps, this last step will not degenerate into a spiritual "shopping list." Too often, when we think of prayer, our minds rush immediately to supplication because we have not cultivated the practice of adoration, confession, and thanksgiving. Supplication by itself can become selfish, but when it follows our adoration, confession, and thanksgiving, it balances our prayer life.

WHAT TO PRAY

Nine times in John's Gospel Jesus commands us to "ask" in prayer. Supplication is God's idea, not just a result of our need. The Lord wants us to ask certain things of Him. But what should we pray for? In the Scriptures, God indicates what *He* wishes us to pray for:

Self. Pray for personal growth in Christlikeness and a sensitivity to God (Colossians 1:9–10).

Family. Pray for spouse, children, and children's children; pray for an unbroken heritage of love for God (Proverbs 20:7; Isaiah 54:13).

Community. Pray that God will show us our part in the area where we live (Jeremiah 29:7). Pray for a visible witness of unity among God's people in our communities (Philippians 4:2–3).

Church. Pray for a sense of unity in vision and heart. Pray for a desire to please God rather than each other (Philippians 2:1–4).

Church Leadership. Pray for a deep sensitivity to the will of God, clarity of vision, and a desire for personal holiness (Hebrews 13:17; 1 Timothy 5:17). Pray for a deep conviction for one-on-one disciple making (2 Timothy 2:2).

The Nation. Pray for national repentance and a consciousness of who God is (Psalm 33:12; Proverbs 14:34).

Leaders in Government. Pray for wisdom and integrity, and an awareness of their accountability to God (1 Timothy 2:1–2; Romans 13:1).

Nonbelievers. Pray for understanding of salvation, and an openness to the Spirit's promptings. Pray that Christians will be sensitive to the nonbelievers in their lives (1 Timothy 2:1–6).

The Sick. Pray for God's healing or assurance (James 5:14–16).

Those in Prison. Pray for an understanding of Christ's forgiveness. Pray for strength to resist sin, and encouragement against loneliness (Hebrews 13:3; Colossians 4:18).

Children. Pray for the unborn children who face abortion. Pray for those whose lives are shattered by divorce (Malachi 4:6; Matthew 19:14).

A Weekly Prayer Strategy

MONDAY — Family

† Pray for immediate family members (you may want to get actual requests from them individually).

† Pray for friends of family members.

TUESDAY — Church

† Pray for the leadership in your local fellowship.

† Pray for the marriages and families of your church leadership; they are key targets of Satan.

† Pray for specific ministries within your church.

WEDNESDAY — Community

† Pray for community leaders.

† Pray for the churches in your community.

† Pray for Christian endeavors in your community (e.g., evangelism outreaches, pro-life efforts, ministries to the homeless, etc.).

THURSDAY — Nation

† Pray for our President.

† Pray for elected officials from your state.

† Pray for the seminaries that are training our future pastors and Christian leaders.

FRIDAY — World

† Pray for world peace.

† Pray for the missionaries your church supports.

† Pray for nations that are "closed" to the Gospel. (Refer regularly to the "Prayer Concerns Around the World" section at the end of this Journal.)

SATURDAY — Afflicted

† Pray for those ministering in difficult circumstances in developing countries.

† Pray for those in prison.

† Pray for those from your church who are hospitalized or sick.

† Pray for the children affected by divorce.

Ideas

A key element in keeping prayer personal is making it creative. Often, routine is the assassin of effective prayer. Below are some ideas for creative prayer.

† Make a "prayer book" of pictures. This would work well for family, leaders, and missionaries. Often *seeing* people gives us a personal burden as we pray for them.

† Make a list of needy people in your church or neighborhood. Pray for them with your family and explore ways that various family members can reach out to them.

† When praying for the nation and the world, pray about the front-page events of your local newspaper.

† Make a list of all the leaders in your church and their specific areas of ministry. Ask them for specific requests from time to time.

† As you use this Journal and read the suggested Scriptures, keep notes of the needs and people who come to mind and pray for them. Then, think of ways you could help answer each prayer need.

† Have your family find out more about some of the countries listed in the **"Prayer Concerns"** section (page 129). Using sources such as *National Geographic,* do a pictorial display in a scrapbook or on a bulletin board and use that as a focal point for prayer.

† Get a list of all missionaries and organizations your church supports. Many have monthly newsletters that keep you informed so you can pray more specifically. Perhaps pray for one or two missionaries or organizations each month.

Jesus, Thy Blood and Righteousness

Jesus, Thy blood and righteousness
My beauty are, my glorious dress;
'Midst flaming worlds, in these arrayed,
With joy shall I lift up my head.

Bold shall I stand in Thy great day,
For who aught to my charge shall lay?
Fully absolved through these I am,
From sin and fear, from guilt and shame.

Lord, I believe Thy precious blood,
Which at the mercy seat of God
Forever doth for sinners plead,
For me, e'en for my soul, was shed.

Lord, I believe were sinners more
Than sands upon the ocean shore,
Thou hast for all a ransom paid,
For all a full atonement made.*

—Thomas Kelly (1769–1855)

*Public domain

Journal Pages

The following pages consist of journal sections for every day of the year. There is a place provided to record your prayer concerns for each day; remember the recommendation that a short, daily prayer time may be better than occasional, longer commitments. There's also a place to record the answers you receive to your prayers. Try to remember what you prayed for from day to day, and be aware of the different ways God may be answering those prayers.

Notice also the suggested daily Scripture readings, which will take you through the entire New Testament in a year. Prayer is conversation with God, and as you read these passages you can think of them as "conversation openers" between you and God. Let Him speak to you through His Word, then spend some time with Him in prayer. Maybe you'll even find answers to prayer in the suggested daily reading.

Finally, remember the "Prayer Concerns Around the World," listed in the final section of your *Personal Prayer Journal*. The many needs represented can seem overwhelming, yet we must be faithful in prayer, and trust God to meet the needs as He sees fit.

May God bless you as you faithfully seek Him in the fellowship of prayer.

PRAYER CONCERNS
7 FRIDAY

—How can I explain the Gospel to my neighbors?
—Where will we find the money for kids in college?
—Will terrorists strike here?

ANSWERS
Matthew 6:1–18

—had good opportunity today—they listened
—could save on vacation travel
—God will be our refuge

January

JANUARY 2005

S	M	T	W	T	F	S
						1
2	3	4	5	6	7	8
9	10	11	12	13	14	15
16	17	18	19	20	21	22
23/30	24/31	25	26	27	28	29

I pray that out of his glorious riches he may strengthen you with power through his Spirit in your inner being.

—Ephesians 3:16

PRAYER CONCERNS   **ANSWERS**

26 SUNDAY • DECEMBER

_____   _____
_____   _____
_____   _____
_____   _____
_____   _____
_____   _____

27 MONDAY

_____   _____
_____   _____
_____   _____
_____   _____
_____   _____
_____   _____

28 TUESDAY

_____   _____
_____   _____
_____   _____
_____   _____
_____   _____
_____   _____

Do not pray for tasks equal to your powers. Pray for powers equal to your tasks.

—Phillips Brooks

PRAYER CONCERNS

ANSWERS

29 WEDNESDAY

30 THURSDAY

31 FRIDAY

1 SATURDAY • JANUARY

Matthew 1

JANUARY 2005

S	M	T	W	T	F	S
						1
2	3	4	5	6	7	8
9	10	11	12	13	14	15
16	17	18	19	20	21	22
23/30	24/31	25	26	27	28	29

January

Yet not my will, but yours be done.

—Luke 22:42

PRAYER CONCERNS   **ANSWERS**

2 SUNDAY   Matthew 2

3 MONDAY   Matthew 3

4 TUESDAY   Matthew 4

24

The basis of all peace of mind . . . is a cessation of the conflict of two wills—His and ours.

—Charles G. Gordon

PRAYER CONCERNS

ANSWERS

5 WEDNESDAY

Matthew 5:1–26

6 THURSDAY

Matthew 5:27–48

7 FRIDAY

Matthew 6:1–18

8 SATURDAY

Matthew 6:19–34

January

JANUARY 2005

S	M	T	W	T	F	S
						1
2	3	4	5	6	7	8
9	10	11	12	13	14	15
16	17	18	19	20	21	22
23/30	24/31	25	26	27	28	29

The LORD is close to the brokenhearted and saves those who are crushed in spirit.

—Psalm 34:18

PRAYER CONCERNS   **ANSWERS**

9 SUNDAY   Matthew 7

10 MONDAY   Matthew 8:1–17

11 TUESDAY   Matthew 8:18–34

We should be thankful for our tears; they prepare our eyes for a clearer vision of God.

— William A. Ward

PRAYER CONCERNS

ANSWERS

12 WEDNESDAY

Matthew 9:1–17

13 THURSDAY

Matthew 9:18–38

14 FRIDAY

Matthew 10:1–20

15 SATURDAY

Matthew 10:21–42

JANUARY 2005

S	M	T	W	T	F	S
						1
2	3	4	5	6	7	8
9	10	11	12	13	14	15
16	17	18	19	20	21	22
23/30	24/31	25	26	27	28	29

January

When you ask, you do not receive, because you ask with wrong motives, that you may spend what you get on your pleasures.

—James 4:3

PRAYER CONCERNS

ANSWERS

16 SUNDAY

Matthew 11

17 MONDAY

Matthew 12:1–23

18 TUESDAY

Matthew 12:24—50

Keep praying, but be thankful that God's answers are wiser than your prayers!

—William Culbertson

PRAYER CONCERNS

ANSWERS

19 WEDNESDAY

Matthew 13:1–30

20 THURSDAY

Matthew 13:31–58

21 FRIDAY

Matthew 14:1–21

22 SATURDAY

Matthew 14:22–36

JANUARY 2005

S	M	T	W	T	F
2	3	4	5	6	7
9	10	11	12	13	14
16	17	18	19	20	21
23/30	24/31	25	26	27	28

January

God is our refuge and strength, an ever-present help in trouble.

—Psalm 46:1

PRAYER CONCERNS **ANSWERS**

23 SUNDAY Matthew 15:1–20

24 MONDAY Matthew 15:21–39

25 TUESDAY Matthew 16

n the day of prosperity we have many refuges to resort to; in the day of adversity, only one.

—*Horatius Bonar*

PRAYER CONCERNS	ANSWERS
26 WEDNESDAY	Matthew 17
27 THURSDAY	Matthew 18:1–20
28 FRIDAY	Matthew 18:21–35
29 SATURDAY	Matthew 19

February

FEBRUARY 2005

S	M	T	W	T	F	S
		1	2	3	4	
6	7	8	9	10	11	1
13	14	15	16	17	18	1
20	21	22	23	24	25	2
27	28					

From the fullness of his grace we have all received one blessing after another.

—John 1:16

PRAYER CONCERNS

ANSWERS

30 SUNDAY • JANUARY

Matthew 20:1–16

31 MONDAY

Matthew 20:17–34

1 TUESDAY • FEBRUARY

Matthew 21:1–22

God sends no one away empty except those who are full of themselves.

—D. L. Moody

PRAYER CONCERNS	ANSWERS
2 WEDNESDAY	Matthew 21:23–46

3 THURSDAY	Matthew 22:1–22

4 FRIDAY	Matthew 22:23–46

5 SATURDAY	Matthew 23:1–22

FEBRUARY 2005

S	M	T	W	T	F	S
		1	2	3	4	5
6	7	8	9	10	11	1
13	14	15	16	17	18	1
20	21	22	23	24	25	2
27	28					

February

For the eyes of the Lord are on the righteous and his ears are attentive to their prayer.

—1 Peter 3:12

PRAYER CONCERNS **ANSWERS**

6 SUNDAY   Matthew 23:23–39

7 MONDAY   Matthew 24:1–28

8 TUESDAY   Matthew 24:29–51

A good prayer, though often used, is still fresh and fair in the eyes and ears of heaven.

—Thomas Fuller

PRAYER CONCERNS

ANSWERS

9 WEDNESDAY

Matthew 25:1–30

10 THURSDAY

Matthew 25:31–46

11 FRIDAY

Matthew 26:1–25

12 SATURDAY

Matthew 26:26–50

FEBRUARY 2005

S	M	T	W	T	F	S
		1	2	3	4	5
6	7	8	9	10	11	1
13	14	15	16	17	18	1
20	21	22	23	24	25	2
27	28					

February

Do not let any unwholesome talk come out of your mouths, but only what is helpful for building others up according to their needs.

—Ephesians 4:29

PRAYER CONCERNS

13 SUNDAY

ANSWERS

Matthew 26:51–75

14 MONDAY

Matthew 27:1–26

15 TUESDAY

Matthew 27:27–50

Keep your words sweet—you may have to eat them!

PRAYER CONCERNS	ANSWERS
16 WEDNESDAY	Matthew 27:51–66
17 THURSDAY	Matthew 28
18 FRIDAY	Mark 1:1–22
19 SATURDAY	Mark 1:23–45

FEBRUARY 2005

S	M	T	W	T	F	S
		1	2	3	4	5
6	7	8	9	10	11	12
13	14	15	16	17	18	19
20	21	22	23	24	25	26
27	28					

He has showed you, O man, what is good. And what does the LORD require of you? To act justly and to love mercy and to walk humbly with your God.

—Micah 6:8

PRAYER CONCERNS

ANSWERS

20 SUNDAY

Mark 2

21 MONDAY

Mark 3:1–19

22 TUESDAY

Mark 3:20–35

One man cannot hold another man down in the ditch without remaining down in the ditch with him.

—*Booker T. Washington*

PRAYER CONCERNS	ANSWERS
23 WEDNESDAY	Mark 4:1–20
24 THURSDAY	Mark 4:21–41
25 FRIDAY	Mark 5:1–20
26 SATURDAY	Mark 5:21–43

MARCH 2005

S	M	T	W	T	F	S
		1	2	3	4	5
6	7	8	9	10	11	12
13	14	15	16	17	18	19
20	21	22	23	24	25	26
27	28	29	30	31		

Be joyful in hope, patient in affliction, faithful in prayer.

—Romans 12:12

PRAYER CONCERNS   **ANSWERS**

27 SUNDAY • FEBRUARY   Mark 6:1–29

28 MONDAY   Mark 6:30–56

1 TUESDAY • MARCH   Mark 7:1–23

God answers knee-mail.

—*Seen on church sign*

PRAYER CONCERNS   **ANSWERS**

2 WEDNESDAY   Mark 7:24–37

_____   _____
_____   _____
_____   _____
_____   _____
_____   _____

3 THURSDAY   Mark 8:1–21

_____   _____
_____   _____
_____   _____
_____   _____
_____   _____

4 FRIDAY   Mark 8:22–38

_____   _____
_____   _____
_____   _____
_____   _____
_____   _____

5 SATURDAY   Mark 9:1–29

_____   _____
_____   _____
_____   _____
_____   _____
_____   _____

# March

MARCH 2005

S	M	T	W	T	F	S
		1	2	3	4	5
6	7	8	9	10	11	12
13	14	15	16	17	18	19
20	21	22	23	24	25	26
27	28	29	30	31		

Whatever is true, whatever is noble, whatever is right, whatever is pure, whatever is lovely, whatever is admirable . . . think about such things.

—Philippians 4:8

PRAYER CONCERNS	ANSWERS
6 SUNDAY	Mark 9:30–50
7 MONDAY	Mark 10:1–31
8 TUESDAY	Mark 10:32–52

Any fool can criticize, condemn, and complain, and most fools do.

—Benjamin Franklin

PRAYER CONCERNS   **ANSWERS**

9 WEDNESDAY   Mark 11:1–18

10 THURSDAY   Mark 11:19–33

11 FRIDAY   Mark 12:1–27

12 SATURDAY   Mark 12:28–44

S	M	T	W	T	F	S
		1	2	3	4	5
6	7	8	9	10	11	12
13	14	15	16	17	18	19
20	21	22	23	24	25	26
27	28	29	30	31		

If we have food and clothing, we will be content with that.

—1 Timothy 6:8

PRAYER CONCERNS

13 SUNDAY

14 MONDAY

15 TUESDAY

ANSWERS

Mark 13:1–20

Mark 13:21–37

Mark 14:1–26

To have more, desire less.

—Martin Luther

PRAYER CONCERNS

16 WEDNESDAY

ANSWERS

Mark 14:27–53

17 THURSDAY

Mark 14:54–72

18 FRIDAY

Mark 15:1–25

19 SATURDAY

Mark 15:26–47

*March*

MARCH 2005

S	M	T	W	T	F	S
		1	2	3	4	5
6	7	8	9	10	11	1
13	14	15	16	17	18	1
20	21	22	23	24	25	2
27	28	29	30	31		

Give thanks to the LORD, for he is good; his love endures forever.

—Psalm 107:1

PRAYER CONCERNS

ANSWERS

20 SUNDAY

Mark 16

21 MONDAY

Luke 1:1–20

22 TUESDAY

Luke 1:21–38

Those blessings are sweetest that are won with prayers and worn with thanks.

—*Thomas Goodwin*

PRAYER CONCERNS	ANSWERS
23 WEDNESDAY	Luke 1:39–56

| **24** THURSDAY | Luke 1:57–80 |

| **25** FRIDAY | Luke 2:1–24 |

| **26** SATURDAY | Luke 2:25–52 |

MARCH 2005

S	M	T	W	T	F	S
		1	2	3	4	5
6	7	8	9	10	11	12
13	14	15	16	17	18	19
20	21	22	23	24	25	26
27	28	29	30	31		

Bear with each other and forgive whatever grievances you may have against one another. Forgive as the Lord forgave you.

—Colossians 3:13

PRAYER CONCERNS **ANSWERS**

27 SUNDAY   Luke 3

28 MONDAY   Luke 4:1–30

29 TUESDAY   Luke 4:31–44

When a deep injury is done us, we never recover until we forgive.

— Alan Paton

PRAYER CONCERNS

ANSWERS

30 WEDNESDAY

Luke 5:1–16

31 THURSDAY

Luke 5:17–39

1 FRIDAY • APRIL

Luke 6:1–26

2 SATURDAY

Luke 6:27–49

APRIL 2005

S M T W T F S
1 2
3 4 5 6 7 8 9
10 11 12 13 14 15 16
17 18 19 20 21 22 2
24 25 26 27 28 29 30

Dear children, let us not love with words or tongue but with actions and in truth.

—1 John 3:18

PRAYER CONCERNS

3 SUNDAY

4 MONDAY

5 TUESDAY

ANSWERS

Luke 7:1–30

Luke 7:31–50

Luke 8:1–25

Whoever loves much, does much.

—Thomas à Kempis

PRAYER CONCERNS	ANSWERS
6 WEDNESDAY	Luke 8:26–56

| **7** THURSDAY | Luke 9:1–17 |

| **8** FRIDAY | Luke 9:18–36 |

| **9** SATURDAY | Luke 9:37–62 |

April

APRIL 2005

S	M	T	W	T	F	S
					1	2
3	4	5	6	7	8	9
10	11	12	13	14	15	16
17	18	19	20	21	22	23
24	25	26	27	28	29	30

Lord, you have been our dwelling place throughout all generations.

—Psalm 90:1

PRAYER CONCERNS

ANSWERS

10 SUNDAY

Luke 10:1–24

11 MONDAY

Luke 10:25–42

12 TUESDAY

Luke 11:1–28

A soul without prayer is a soul without a home.

—Abraham Joshua Heschel

PRAYER CONCERNS	ANSWERS
13 WEDNESDAY	Luke 11:29–54

14 THURSDAY	Luke 12:1–31

15 FRIDAY	Luke 12:32–59

16 SATURDAY	Luke 13:1–22

April

APRIL 2005

S	M	T	W	T	F	
					1	
3	4	5	6	7	8	
10	11	12	13	14	15	1
17	18	19	20	21	22	2
24	25	26	27	28	29	3

For whoever wants to save his life will lose it, but whoever loses his life for me will find it.

—Matthew 16:25

PRAYER CONCERNS

ANSWERS

17 SUNDAY

Luke 13:23–35

18 MONDAY

Luke 14:1–24

19 TUESDAY

Luke 14:25–35

Seek joy in what you give, not in what you get.

—Author unknown

PRAYER CONCERNS	ANSWERS
20 WEDNESDAY	Luke 15:1–10
21 THURSDAY	Luke 15:11–32
22 FRIDAY	Luke 16
23 SATURDAY	Luke 17:1–19

APRIL 2005

S	M	T	W	T	F	S
					1	
3	4	5	6	7	8	
10	11	12	13	14	15	
17	18	19	20	21	22	
24	25	26	27	28	29	3

April

The prayer of a righteous man is powerful and effective.

—James 5:16

PRAYER CONCERNS	ANSWERS
24 SUNDAY	Luke 17:20–37
25 MONDAY	Luke 18:1–23
26 TUESDAY	Luke 18:24–43

I would rather teach one man to pray than ten men to preach.

—J. H. Jowett

PRAYER CONCERNS   **ANSWERS**

27 WEDNESDAY   Luke 19:1–27

_____   _____
_____   _____
_____   _____
_____   _____
_____   _____
_____   _____

28 THURSDAY   Luke 19:28–48

_____   _____
_____   _____
_____   _____
_____   _____
_____   _____
_____   _____

29 FRIDAY   Luke 20:1–26

_____   _____
_____   _____
_____   _____
_____   _____
_____   _____
_____   _____

30 SATURDAY   Luke 20:27–47

_____   _____
_____   _____
_____   _____
_____   _____
_____   _____
_____   _____

MAY 2005

S	M	T	W	T	F	
1	2	3	4	5	6	
8	9	10	11	12	13	
15	16	17	18	19	20	
22	23	24	25	26	27	
29	30	31				

Do not love sleep or you will grow poor; stay awake and you will have food to spare.

—Proverbs 20:13

PRAYER CONCERNS　　　　　　　**ANSWERS**

1 SUNDAY　　　　　　　　Luke 21:1–19

2 MONDAY　　　　　　　　Luke 21:20–38

3 TUESDAY　　　　　　　Luke 22:1–20

An ant on the move does more than a dozing ox.

—*Mexican proverb*

PRAYER CONCERNS	ANSWERS
4 WEDNESDAY	Luke 22:21–46
5 THURSDAY	Luke 22:47–71
6 FRIDAY	Luke 23:1–25
7 SATURDAY	Luke 23:26–56

 *May*

MAY 2005

S	M	T	W	T	F
1	2	3	4	5	6
8	9	10	11	12	13	1
15	16	17	18	19	20	2
22	23	24	25	26	27	2
29	30	31			

For I was hungry and you gave me something to eat, I was thirsty and you gave me something to drink, I was a stranger and you invited me in.

—Matthew 25:35

PRAYER CONCERNS

8 SUNDAY

9 MONDAY

10 TUESDAY

ANSWERS

Luke 24:1–35

Luke 24:36–53

John 1:1–28

I can't do everything, but that won't stop me from doing the little I can do.

—Everett Hale

PRAYER CONCERNS	ANSWERS
11 WEDNESDAY	John 1:29–51
12 THURSDAY	John 2
13 FRIDAY	John 3:1–18
14 SATURDAY	John 3:19–36

MAY 2005

S	M	T	W	T	F	S
	1	2	3	4	5	6	7
8	9	10	11	12	13	14
15	16	17	18	19	20	21
22	23	24	25	26	27	28
29	30	31				

My God will meet all your needs according to his glorious riches in Christ Jesus.

—Philippians 4:19

PRAYER CONCERNS

ANSWERS

15 SUNDAY

John 4:1–30

16 MONDAY

John 4:31–54

17 TUESDAY

John 5:1–24

In labors of love, every day is payday.

—Gaines Brewster

PRAYER CONCERNS	ANSWERS

18 WEDNESDAY — John 5:25–47

19 THURSDAY — John 6:1–21

20 FRIDAY — John 6:22–44

21 SATURDAY — John 6:45–71

May

MAY 2005

S	M	T	W	T	F	S
1	2	3	4	5	6	7
8	9	10	11	12	13	1
15	16	17	18	19	20	2
22	23	24	25	26	27	2
29	30	31				

Pray in the Spirit on all occasions with all kinds of prayers and requests.
—Ephesians 6:18

PRAYER CONCERNS

ANSWERS

22 SUNDAY

John 7:1–27

_____

_____

_____

_____

_____

23 MONDAY

John 7:28–53

_____

_____

_____

_____

_____

24 TUESDAY

John 8:1–27

_____

_____

_____

_____

_____

You can only pray all the time everywhere if you bother to pray some of
the time somewhere.

—J. Dalrymple

PRAYER CONCERNS   **ANSWERS**

25 WEDNESDAY   John 8:28–59

26 THURSDAY   John 9:1–23

27 FRIDAY   John 9:24–41

28 SATURDAY   John 10:1–23

MAY 2005

S	M	T	W	T	F
1	2	3	4	5	6
8	9	10	11	12	13
15	16	17	18	19	20
22	23	24	25	26	27
29	30	31			

In everything, do to others what you would have them do to you, for this sums up the Law and the Prophets.

—Matthew 7:12

PRAYER CONCERNS

ANSWERS

29 SUNDAY

John 10:24–42

30 MONDAY

John 11:1–29

31 TUESDAY

John 11:30–57

The smile you send out returns to you.

—*Indian proverb*

PRAYER CONCERNS	ANSWERS
1 WEDNESDAY • JUNE	John 12:1–26
2 THURSDAY	John 12:27–50
3 FRIDAY	John 13:1–20
4 SATURDAY	John 13:21–38

June

JUNE 2005

S	M	T	W	T	F	S
			1	2	3	4
5	6	7	8	9	10	1
12	13	14	15	16	17	1
19	20	21	22	23	24	2
26	27	28	29	30		

Lazy hands make a man poor, but diligent hands bring wealth.

—Proverbs 10:4

PRAYER CONCERNS

ANSWERS

5 SUNDAY

John 14

6 MONDAY

John 15

7 TUESDAY

John 16

68

The world is filled with willing people; some willing to work, the rest willing to let them.

—Robert Frost

PRAYER CONCERNS	ANSWERS
8 WEDNESDAY	John 17

PRAYER CONCERNS	ANSWERS
9 THURSDAY	John 18:1–18

PRAYER CONCERNS	ANSWERS
10 FRIDAY	John 18:19–40

PRAYER CONCERNS	ANSWERS
11 SATURDAY	John 19:1–22

JUNE 2005

S	M	T	W	T	F	S
			1	2	3	4
5	6	7	8	9	10	11
12	13	14	15	16	17	18
19	20	21	22	23	24	25
26	27	28	29	30		

It is good to praise the LORD and make music to your name, O Most High, to proclaim your love in the morning and your faithfulness at night.

—Psalm 92:1–2

PRAYER CONCERNS

ANSWERS

12 SUNDAY

John 19:23–42

13 MONDAY

John 20

14 TUESDAY

John 21

Every time that is not seized upon by some other duty is seasonable enough for prayer.

—Jeremy Taylor

PRAYER CONCERNS	ANSWERS
15 WEDNESDAY	Acts 1

16 THURSDAY	Acts 2:1–21

17 FRIDAY	Acts 2:22–47

18 SATURDAY	Acts 3

June

JUNE 2005

S	M	T	W	T	F	S
			1	2	3	4
5	6	7	8	9	10	11
12	13	14	15	16	17	18
19	20	21	22	23	24	25
26	27	28	29	30		

Sell your possessions and give to the poor. Provide purses for yourselves that will not wear out, a treasure in heaven that will not be exhausted.

—Luke 12:33

PRAYER CONCERNS

ANSWERS

19 SUNDAY

Acts 4:1–22

20 MONDAY

Acts 4:23–37

21 TUESDAY

Acts 5:1–21

Nothing that is God's is obtainable by money.

—Tertullian

PRAYER CONCERNS	ANSWERS
22 WEDNESDAY	Acts 5:22–42
23 THURSDAY	Acts 6
24 FRIDAY	Acts 7:1–21
25 SATURDAY	Acts 7:22–43

JUNE 2005

S	M	T	W	T	F	S
			1	2	3	4
5	6	7	8	9	10	11
12	13	14	15	16	17	18
19	20	21	22	23	24	25
26	27	28	29	30		

Pride goes before destruction, a haughty spirit before a fall.

—Proverbs 16:18

PRAYER CONCERNS   **ANSWERS**

26 SUNDAY   Acts 7:44–60

27 MONDAY   Acts 8:1–25

28 TUESDAY   Acts 8:26–40

There was one who thought he was above me, and he **was** above me until he had that thought.

—Elbert Hubbard

PRAYER CONCERNS

ANSWERS

29 WEDNESDAY

Acts 9:1–21

30 THURSDAY

Acts 9:22–43

1 FRIDAY • JULY

Acts 10:1–23

2 SATURDAY

Acts 10:24–48

JULY 2005

S	M	T	W	T	F	S
					1	2
3	4	5	6	7	8	9
10	11	12	13	14	15	16
17	18	19	20	21	22	23
24/31	25	26	27	28	29	30

July

I cry aloud to the LORD; I lift up my voice to the LORD for mercy. I pour out my complaint before him; before him I tell my trouble.

—Psalm 142:1–2

PRAYER CONCERNS   **ANSWERS**

3 SUNDAY   Acts 11

4 MONDAY   Acts 12

5 TUESDAY   Acts 13:1–25

Prayer is nothing else than the opening up of our heart before God.

—John Calvin

PRAYER CONCERNS	ANSWERS
6 WEDNESDAY	Acts 13:26–52
7 THURSDAY	Acts 14
8 FRIDAY	Acts 15:1–21
9 SATURDAY	Acts 15:22–41

July

JULY 2005

S	M	T	W	T	F	S
					1	2
3	4	5	6	7	8	9
10	11	12	13	14	15	16
17	18	19	20	21	22	23
24/31	25	26	27	28	29	30

Blessed is he whose transgressions are forgiven, whose sins are covered. Blessed is the man whose sin the LORD does not count against him and in whose spirit is no deceit.

—Psalm 32:1–2

PRAYER CONCERNS

ANSWERS

10 SUNDAY

Acts 16:1–21

11 MONDAY

Acts 16:22–40

12 TUESDAY

Acts 17:1–15

There is no pillow so soft as a clear conscience.

—French proverb

PRAYER CONCERNS

ANSWERS

13 WEDNESDAY

Acts 17:16–34

14 THURSDAY

Acts 18

15 FRIDAY

Acts 19:1–20

16 SATURDAY

Acts 19:21–41

July

JULY 2005

S	M	T	W	T	F	S
					1	2
3	4	5	6	7	8	9
10	11	12	13	14	15	1
17	18	19	20	21	22	2
24/31	25	26	27	28	29	3

Do not let this Book of the Law depart from your mouth; meditate on it day and night, so that you may be careful to do everything written in it. Then you will be prosperous and successful.

—Joshua 1:8

PRAYER CONCERNS

ANSWERS

17 SUNDAY

Acts 20:1–16

18 MONDAY

Acts 20:17–38

19 TUESDAY

Acts 21:1–17

The time is always right to do what is right.

—Martin Luther King, Jr.

PRAYER CONCERNS	ANSWERS
20 WEDNESDAY	Acts 21:18–40

| **21** THURSDAY | Acts 22 |

| **22** FRIDAY | Acts 23:1–15 |

| **23** SATURDAY | Acts 23:16–35 |

JULY 2005

S	M	T	W	T	F	S
					1	2
3	4	5	6	7	8	9
10	11	12	13	14	15	16
17	18	19	20	21	22	23
24/31	25	26	27	28	29	30

Cast all your anxiety on him because he cares for you.

—1 Peter 5:7

PRAYER CONCERNS

ANSWERS

24 SUNDAY

Acts 24

25 MONDAY

Acts 25

26 TUESDAY

Acts 26

The way to worry about nothing is to pray about everything.

—Author unknown

PRAYER CONCERNS

ANSWERS

27 WEDNESDAY

Acts 27:1–26

28 THURSDAY

Acts 27:27–44

29 FRIDAY

Acts 28

30 SATURDAY

Romans 1

AUGUST 2005

S	M	T	W	T	F	S
	1	2	3	4	5	6
7	8	9	10	11	12	13
14	15	16	17	18	19	20
21	22	23	24	25	26	27
28	29	30	31			

The love of money is a root of all kinds of evil. Some people, eager for money, have wandered from the faith and pierced themselves with many griefs.

—1 Timothy 6:10

PRAYER CONCERNS

31 SUNDAY • JULY

1 MONDAY • AUGUST

2 TUESDAY

ANSWERS

Romans 2

Romans 3

Romans 4

He that serves God for money will serve the Devil for better wages.

—*Roger L'Estrange*

PRAYER CONCERNS	ANSWERS
3 WEDNESDAY	Romans 5
4 THURSDAY	Romans 6
5 FRIDAY	Romans 7
6 SATURDAY	Romans 8:1–21

August

S	M	T	W	T	F	S
	1	2	3	4	5	6
7	8	9	10	11	12	1
14	15	16	17	18	19	2
21	22	23	24	25	26	2
28	29	30	31			

Love each other as I have loved you.

—John 15:12

PRAYER CONCERNS

ANSWERS

7 SUNDAY

Romans 8:22–39

8 MONDAY

Romans 9:1–15

9 TUESDAY

Romans 9:16–33

No one is useless in this world who lightens the burden of it for anyone else.

—*Charles Dickens*

PRAYER CONCERNS	ANSWERS
10 WEDNESDAY	Romans 10

11 THURSDAY	Romans 11:1–18

12 FRIDAY	Romans 11:19–36

13 SATURDAY	Romans 12

AUGUST 2005

S	M	T	W	T	F	
	1	2	3	4	5	
7	8	9	10	11	12	1
14	15	16	17	18	19	2
21	22	23	24	25	26	2
28	29	30	31			

August

Trust in the LORD with all your heart and lean not on your own understanding; in all your ways acknowledge him, and he will make your paths straight.

—Proverbs 3:5–6

PRAYER CONCERNS

ANSWERS

14 SUNDAY

Romans 13

15 MONDAY

Romans 14

16 TUESDAY

Romans 15:1–13

None live so easily, so pleasantly, as those that live by faith.

—Matthew Henry

PRAYER CONCERNS

ANSWERS

17 WEDNESDAY

Romans 15:14–33

18 THURSDAY

Romans 16

19 FRIDAY

1 Corinthians 1

20 SATURDAY

1 Corinthians 2

August

AUGUST 2005

S	M	T	W	T	F
	1	2	3	4	5
7	8	9	10	11	12
14	15	16	17	18	19
21	22	23	24	25	26
28	29	30	31		

Very early in the morning, while it was still dark, Jesus got up, left the house and went off to a solitary place, where he prayed.

—Mark 1:35

PRAYER CONCERNS	**ANSWERS**
21 SUNDAY	1 Corinthians 3

22 MONDAY	1 Corinthians 4

23 TUESDAY	1 Corinthians 5

It is remarked of Old Testament saints, that they rose early in the morning; and particularly of our Lord, that he rose a great while before day to pray. The morning befriends devotion.

—*George Whitefield*

PRAYER CONCERNS

ANSWERS

24 WEDNESDAY

1 Corinthians 6

25 THURSDAY

1 Corinthians 7:1–19

26 FRIDAY

1 Corinthians 7:20–40

27 SATURDAY

1 Corinthians 8

August

AUGUST 2005

S	M	T	W	T	F	S
	1	2	3	4	5	6
7	8	9	10	11	12	1
14	15	16	17	18	19	2
21	22	23	24	25	26	2
28	29	30	31			

I am not ashamed of the gospel, because it is the power of God for the salvation of everyone who believes.

—Romans 1:16

PRAYER CONCERNS

ANSWERS

28 SUNDAY

1 Corinthians 9

29 MONDAY

1 Corinthians 10:1–18

30 TUESDAY

1 Corinthians 10:19–33

The Christian faith is not true because it works. It works because it is true.

—*Os Guinness*

PRAYER CONCERNS	ANSWERS
31 WEDNESDAY	1 Corinthians 11:1–16

1 THURSDAY • SEPTEMBER	1 Corinthians 11:17–34

2 FRIDAY	1 Corinthians 12

3 SATURDAY	1 Corinthians 13

SEPTEMBER 2005

S	M	T	W	T	F	S
				1	2	3
4	5	6	7	8	9	1O
11	12	13	14	15	16	17
18	19	20	21	22	23	24
25	26	27	28	29	30	

September

Faith by itself, if it is not accompanied by action, is dead.

—James 2:17

PRAYER CONCERNS

ANSWERS

4 SUNDAY

1 Corinthians 14:1–20

5 MONDAY

1 Corinthians 14:21–40

6 TUESDAY

1 Corinthians 15:1–28

It is no use walking anywhere to preach unless our walking is our preaching.

—*Francis of Assisi*

PRAYER CONCERNS	ANSWERS
7 WEDNESDAY	1 Corinthians 15:29–58
8 THURSDAY	1 Corinthians 16
9 FRIDAY	2 Corinthians 1
10 SATURDAY	2 Corinthians 2

SEPTEMBER 2005

S	M	T	W	T	F	S
				1	2	3
4	5	6	7	8	9	10
11	12	13	14	15	16	17
18	19	20	21	22	23	24
25	26	27	28	29	30	

September

Far be it from me that I should sin against the LORD by failing to pray for you.

—1 Samuel 12:23

PRAYER CONCERNS

11 SUNDAY

12 MONDAY

13 TUESDAY

ANSWERS

2 Corinthians 3

2 Corinthians 4

2 Corinthians 5

Heaven is full of answers to prayers for which no one ever bothered to ask.

—Billy Graham

PRAYER CONCERNS	ANSWERS
14 WEDNESDAY	2 Corinthians 6
15 THURSDAY	2 Corinthians 7
16 FRIDAY	2 Corinthians 8
17 SATURDAY	2 Corinthians 9

September

SEPTEMBER 2005

S	M	T	W	T	F	S
				1	2	3
4	5	6	7	8	9	10
11	12	13	14	15	16	17
18	19	20	21	22	23	24
25	26	27	28	29	30	

Delight yourself in the LORD and he will give you the desires of your heart.

—Psalm 37:4

PRAYER CONCERNS

18 SUNDAY

19 MONDAY

20 TUESDAY

ANSWERS

2 Corinthians 10

2 Corinthians 11:1–15

2 Corinthians 11:16–33

It is not how much we have, but how much we enjoy, that makes happiness.

—Charles H. Spurgeon

PRAYER CONCERNS	ANSWERS
21 WEDNESDAY	2 Corinthians 12
22 THURSDAY	2 Corinthians 13
23 FRIDAY	Galatians 1
24 SATURDAY	Galatians 2

SEPTEMBER 2005

S	M	T	W	T	F	S
				1	2	3
4	5	6	7	8	9	10
11	12	13	14	15	16	17
18	19	20	21	22	23	24
25	26	27	28	29	30	

Above all, love each other deeply, because love covers over a multitude of sins.

—1 Peter 4:8

PRAYER CONCERNS   **ANSWERS**

25 SUNDAY   Galatians 3

26 MONDAY   Galatians 4

27 TUESDAY   Galatians 5

Many a man expects his wife to be perfect and to understand why he isn't.

—Author unknown

PRAYER CONCERNS	ANSWERS
28 WEDNESDAY	Galatians 6

_____

| **29** THURSDAY | Ephesians 1 |

_____

| **30** FRIDAY | Ephesians 2 |

_____

| **1** SATURDAY • OCTOBER | Ephesians 3 |

OCTOBER 2005

S M T W T F S
                    1
2 3 4 5 6 7 8
9 10 11 12 13 14 15
16 17 18 19 20 21 22
23/30 24/31 25 26 27 28 29

October

But as for me, it is good to be near God. I have made the Sovereign LORD my refuge.

—Psalm 73:28

PRAYER CONCERNS	ANSWERS
2 SUNDAY	Ephesians 4

PRAYER CONCERNS	ANSWERS
3 MONDAY	Ephesians 5:1–16

PRAYER CONCERNS	ANSWERS
4 TUESDAY	Ephesians 5:17–33

Strictly speaking there is really only one legitimate object in prayer, and that is the desire for communion with God.

—*A. Victor Murray*

PRAYER CONCERNS	ANSWERS
5 WEDNESDAY	Ephesians 6
6 THURSDAY	Philippians 1
7 FRIDAY	Philippians 2
8 SATURDAY	Philippians 3

OCTOBER 2005

S	M	T	W	T	F	S
						1
2	3	4	5	6	7	8
9	10	11	12	13	14	15
16	17	18	19	20	21	22
23/30	24/31	25	26	27	28	29

October

Who is a God like you, who pardons sin and forgives the transgression of the remnant of his inheritance? You do not stay angry forever but delight to show mercy.

—Micah 7:18

PRAYER CONCERNS

ANSWERS

9 SUNDAY

Philippians 4

10 MONDAY

Colossians 1

11 TUESDAY

Colossians 2

God's love for poor sinners is very wonderful, but God's patience with ill-natured saints is a deeper mystery.

—Henry Drummond

PRAYER CONCERNS	ANSWERS
12 WEDNESDAY	Colossians 3
13 THURSDAY	Colossians 4
14 FRIDAY	1 Thessalonians 1
15 SATURDAY	1 Thessalonians 2

October

OCTOBER 2005

S	M	T	W	T	F	S
						1
2	3	4	5	6	7	8
9	10	11	12	13	14	15
16	17	18	19	20	21	22
23/30	24/31	25	26	27	28	29

If he sins against you seven times in a day, and seven times comes back to you and says, "I repent," forgive him.

—Luke 17:4

PRAYER CONCERNS

ANSWERS

16 SUNDAY

1 Thessalonians 3

17 MONDAY

1 Thessalonians 4

18 TUESDAY

1 Thessalonians 5

Everyone says forgiveness is a lovely idea, until they have something to forgive.

—*C. S. Lewis*

PRAYER CONCERNS	ANSWERS
19 WEDNESDAY	2 Thessalonians 1
20 THURSDAY	2 Thessalonians 2
21 FRIDAY	2 Thessalonians 3
22 SATURDAY	1 Timothy 1

October

OCTOBER 2005

S	M	T	W	T	F	S
						1
2	3	4	5	6	7	8
9	10	11	12	13	14	15
16	17	18	19	20	21	22
23/30	24/31	25	26	27	28	29

I pray also that the eyes of your heart may be enlightened.

—Ephesians 1:18

PRAYER CONCERNS

ANSWERS

23 SUNDAY

1 Timothy 2

24 MONDAY

1 Timothy 3

25 TUESDAY

1 Timothy 4

You can only understand Scripture on your knees.

—Maurice Zundel

PRAYER CONCERNS

ANSWERS

26 WEDNESDAY

1 Timothy 5

27 THURSDAY

1 Timothy 6

28 FRIDAY

2 Timothy 1

29 SATURDAY

2 Timothy 2

November

NOVEMBER 2005

S	M	T	W	T	F	S
		1	2	3	4	5
6	7	8	9	10	11	12
13	14	15	16	17	18	19
20	21	22	23	24	25	26
27	28	29	30			

We pray this in order that you may live a life worthy of the Lord and may please him in every way: bearing fruit in every good work, growing in the knowledge of God.

—Colossians 1:10

PRAYER CONCERNS

ANSWERS

30 SUNDAY • OCTOBER

2 Timothy 3

31 MONDAY

2 Timothy 4

1 TUESDAY • NOVEMBER

Titus 1

Whatever God gives you to do, do it as well as you can. This is the best possible preparation for what he may want you to do next.

—George Macdonald

PRAYER CONCERNS	**ANSWERS**
2 WEDNESDAY	Titus 2
3 THURSDAY	Titus 3
4 FRIDAY	Philemon
5 SATURDAY	Hebrews 1

NOVEMBER 2005

S	M	T	W	T	F	S
		1	2	3	4	5
6	7	8	9	10	11	12
13	14	15	16	17	18	19
20	21	22	23	24	25	26
27	28	29	30			

November

With God all things are possible.

—Matthew 19:26

PRAYER CONCERNS

ANSWERS

6 SUNDAY

Hebrews 2

7 MONDAY

Hebrews 3

8 TUESDAY

Hebrews 4

You never test the resources of God until you attempt the impossible.

—*F. B. Meyer*

PRAYER CONCERNS   **ANSWERS**

9 WEDNESDAY   Hebrews 5

10 THURSDAY   Hebrews 6

11 FRIDAY   Hebrews 7

12 SATURDAY   Hebrews 8

NOVEMBER 2005

S	M	T	W	T	F	S
		1	2	3	4	5
6	7	8	9	10	11	12
13	14	15	16	17	18	19
20	21	22	23	24	25	26
27	28	29	30			

November

"Martha, Martha," the Lord answered, "you are worried and upset about many things, but only one thing is needed. Mary has chosen what is better, and it will not be taken away from her."

—Luke 10:41–42

PRAYER CONCERNS

13 SUNDAY

14 MONDAY

15 TUESDAY

ANSWERS

Hebrews 9

Hebrews 10:1–18

Hebrews 10:19–39

Our greatest danger in life is in permitting the urgent things to crowd out the important.

—Charles E. Hummel

PRAYER CONCERNS

ANSWERS

16 WEDNESDAY

Hebrews 11

17 THURSDAY

Hebrews 12

18 FRIDAY

Hebrews 13

19 SATURDAY

James 1

November

NOVEMBER 2005

S	M	T	W	T	F	S
		1	2	3	4	5
6	7	8	9	10	11	12
13	14	15	16	17	18	19
20	21	22	23	24	25	26
27	28	29	30			

Thanks be to God! He gives us the victory through our Lord Jesus Christ.

—1 Corinthians 15:57

PRAYER CONCERNS

ANSWERS

20 SUNDAY

James 2

21 MONDAY

James 3

22 TUESDAY

James 4

Thou hast given so much to me. . . . Give one thing more—a grateful heart.

—George Herbert

PRAYER CONCERNS

23 WEDNESDAY

24 THURSDAY

25 FRIDAY

26 SATURDAY

ANSWERS

James 5

1 Peter 1

1 Peter 2

1 Peter 3

NOVEMBER 2005

S	M	T	W	T	F	S
		1	2	3	4	5
6	7	8	9	10	11	12
13	14	15	16	17	18	19
20	21	22	23	24	25	26
27	28	29	30			

Because he himself suffered when he was tempted, he is able to help those who are being tempted.

—Hebrews 2:18

PRAYER CONCERNS   **ANSWERS**

27 SUNDAY   1 Peter 4

28 MONDAY   1 Peter 5

29 TUESDAY   2 Peter 1

Some temptations come to the industrious, but all temptations attack the idle.

—Charles H. Spurgeon

PRAYER CONCERNS	ANSWERS
30 WEDNESDAY	2 Peter 2
1 THURSDAY • DECEMBER	2 Peter 3
2 FRIDAY	1 John 1
3 SATURDAY	1 John 2

DECEMBER 2005

S	M	T	W	T	F	S
				1	2	3
4	5	6	7	8	9	10
11	12	13	14	15	16	17
18	19	20	21	22	23	24
25	26	27	28	29	30	31

December

The eternal God is your refuge, and underneath are the everlasting arms.

—Deuteronomy 33:27

PRAYER CONCERNS

ANSWERS

4 SUNDAY

1 John 3

5 MONDAY

1 John 4

6 TUESDAY

1 John 5

How calmly may we commit ourselves to the hands of him who bears up the world.

—Jean Paul Richter

PRAYER CONCERNS	ANSWERS
7 WEDNESDAY	2 John

8 THURSDAY	3 John

9 FRIDAY	Jude

10 SATURDAY	Revelation 1

DECEMBER 2005

S	M	T	W	T	F	S
				1	2	3
4	5	6	7	8	9	10
11	12	13	14	15	16	17
18	19	20	21	22	23	24
25	26	27	28	29	30	31

Be joyful always; pray continually; give thanks in all circumstances, for this is God's will for you in Christ Jesus.

—1 Thessalonians 5:16–18

PRAYER CONCERNS

ANSWERS

11 SUNDAY

Revelation 2

12 MONDAY

Revelation 3

13 TUESDAY

Revelation 4

Is prayer your steering wheel or your spare tire?

—Corrie ten Boom

PRAYER CONCERNS

ANSWERS

14 WEDNESDAY

Revelation 5

15 THURSDAY

Revelation 6

16 FRIDAY

Revelation 7

17 SATURDAY

Revelation 8

DECEMBER 2005

S	M	T	W	T	F	S
				1	2	3
4	5	6	7	8	9	10
11	12	13	14	15	16	1
18	19	20	21	22	23	2
25	26	27	28	29	30	3

If anyone says, "I love God," yet hates his brother, he is a liar. For anyone who does not love his brother, whom he has seen, cannot love God, whom he has not seen.

—1 John 4:20

PRAYER CONCERNS

18 SUNDAY

ANSWERS

Revelation 9

19 MONDAY

Revelation 10

20 TUESDAY

Revelation 11

The Bible tells us to love our neighbors, and also to love our enemies;
probably because they are generally the same people.

—G. K. Chesterton

PRAYER CONCERNS   **ANSWERS**

21 WEDNESDAY   Revelation 12

22 THURSDAY   Revelation 13

23 FRIDAY   Revelation 14

24 SATURDAY   Revelation 15

DECEMBER 2005

S	M	T	W	T	F	S
				1	2	3
4	5	6	7	8	9	1
11	12	13	14	15	16	1
18	19	20	21	22	23	2
25	26	27	28	29	30	3

Therefore, prepare your minds for action; be self-controlled; set your hope fully on the grace to be given you when Jesus Christ is revealed.

—1 Peter 1:13

PRAYER CONCERNS

ANSWERS

25 SUNDAY

Revelation 16

26 MONDAY

Revelation 17

27 TUESDAY

Revelation 18

Our duty as Christians is always to keep heaven in our eye and earth under our feet.

—*Matthew Henry*

PRAYER CONCERNS

28 WEDNESDAY

29 THURSDAY

30 FRIDAY

31 SATURDAY

ANSWERS

Revelation 19

Revelation 20

Revelation 21

Revelation 22

around the world

Prayer Concerns

Afghanistan

AFGHANISTAN has been a primary focus of the international war on terror since September 11, 2001. Just as important as military operations is the effort to revive the nation's economy, which had drifted toward illegal drug trafficking to support the terrorists. **PRAY** that this nation will once again see economic prosperity and peace. Pray for those who seek to proclaim Christ while helping the nation in its recovery.

Population: 28,717,000*
Capital: Kabul
Language: Pushtu, Dari Persian**
Literacy: 25%***
Income (GDP) per capita: $700****
Religions: Muslim 98%, Parsee 1%*****

Albania

Under communism in **ALBANIA**, hundreds of Christian churches were destroyed, and anyone caught carrying a Bible was imprisoned. Today, thousands are responding to the gospel, and there is a church meeting in the former home of the communist dictator! **PRAY** for the rebuilding of churches, and of God's eternal kingdom in the hearts and minds of Albania.

Population: 3,582,000
Capital: Tirana
Language: Albanian, Greek
Literacy: 92%
Income (GDP) per capita: $4,500
Religions: Muslim 39%, Orthodox 24%,
     nonreligious 19%, Catholic 17%

*Based on *The New York Times 2004 Almanac.*
**Only the one or two most predominant languages are reported.
***Based on *Operation World (2001).*
****Based on *The New York Times 2004 Almanac.* Per capita income is here stated as Gross Domestic Product (GDP) per capita. In many developing nations where wealth is unevenly distributed, actual average household income may be much lower than the stated GDP per capita.
*****Adapted from *Operation World (2001).* Amounts of less than 1% not reported.

Algeria

The Internet has become an effective means of evangelization in nations such as **ALGERIA** that traditionally have been closed to Christian missions. Just one web site reports that people from 127 nations are taking the Bible correspondence courses they offer. **PRAY** that those who find salvation through such Internet ministries will also receive instruction in Christian living and will find fellowship with real, live Christians!

Population: 32,819,000
Capital: Algiers
Language: Arabic, French
Literacy: 62%
Income (GDP) per capita: $5,300
Religions: Muslim 96%,
   nonreligious 3%

Angola

As **ANGOLA** continues to recover from decades of civil warfare, its cities are filled with refugees, including many abandoned children. The church has thrived amid these desperate circumstances. **PRAY** that the churches would lead the way to recovery, that they would be able to provide homes for the homeless, and that many more in Angola would find the eternal security of salvation through Jesus Christ.

Population: 10,767,000
Capital: Luanda
Language: Bantu, Portuguese
Literacy: 35%
Income (GDP) per capita: $1,600
Religions: Catholic 62%,
   Protestant 18%, various Christian 13%,
   traditional/indigenous 5%,
   marginal Christian 1%

Argentina

For many years a prosperous nation, **ARGENTINA** has recently fallen on hard times. Things became so bad in Buenos Aires in 2003 that lawmakers voted to legalize trash scavenging, to help some of its poorest people support themselves. **PRAY** for those who suffer during such times. Pray for good leadership at all levels of government. And pray that the challenges they face will turn many to Christ.

Population: 38,741,000
Capital: Buenos Aires
Language: Spanish, English
Literacy: 95%
Income (GDP) per capita: $10,200
Religions: Catholic 88%, Protestant 6%,
    nonreligious 3%, Jewish 1%, Muslim 1%

Australia

On the one hand, Christianity in **AUSTRALIA** faces the challenge of the 28 percent of Australians who consider themselves "nonreligious." At the other extreme, radical Muslims are recruiting Aboriginal young people to join their ranks. **PRAY** for those who faithfully proclaim Christ as they face these and many other challenges.

Population: 19,732,000
Capital: Canberra
Language: English
Literacy: 99%
Income (GDP) per capita: $27,000
Religions: nonreligious 28%,
    Catholic 25%, Anglican 20%,
    Protestant 13%, various Christian 6%,
    Orthodox 3%, Muslim 2%, Buddhist 1%,
    marginal Christian 1%

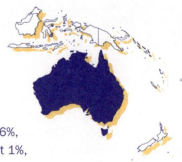

around the world

Prayer Concerns

Azerbaijan

AZERBAIJAN is developing its oil reserves, and its per capita income seems relatively high. But much of its wealth goes to people connected with the corrupt government, while most people live in poverty. **PRAY** for prosperity for all Azerbaijanis. Pray for effective presentation of the Gospel in this land where Christianity is viewed as the religion of Armenia, a bitter rival.

Population: 7,831,000
Capital: Baku
Language: Azeri
Literacy: 97%
Income (GDP) per capita: $3,500
Religions: Muslim 83%,
   nonreligious 11%, Orthodox 4%

Belarus

In 2003, the president of **BELARUS,** widely known as Europe's last dictator, signed a pact with leaders of the Orthodox Church that guaranteed the preservation of communist ideology in government and placed tight restrictions on evangelical Christian churches and other religious groups. **PRAY** that the Gospel would continue to be clearly proclaimed in these difficult circumstances.

Population: 10,322,000
Capital: Minsk
Language: Byelorusian, Russian
Literacy: 98%
Income (GDP) per capita: $8,200
Religions: Orthodox 48%,
   nonreligious 20%,
   various Christian 16%,
   Catholic 13%, Protestant 1%,
   Jewish 1%

Brazil

An estimated 6,500 "Ibero-Americans" (Latin Americans, Portuguese, Spaniards, and North American Hispanics) serve as missionaries in Africa, the Middle East, and Asia. **BRAZIL** is a major sending nation. Ibero-Americans often serve in areas where missionaries from the United States are not welcome. **PRAY** for the faithfulness and increase of this mighty new force in world missions.

Population: 182,033,000
Capital: Brasília
Language: Portuguese
Literacy: 83%
Income (GDP) per capita: $7,600
Religions: Catholic 73%, various Christian 9%,
    Protestant 7%, traditional/indigenous 5%,
    nonreligious 3%, marginal Christian 1%

Bulgaria

An estimated 15 percent of college graduates leave **BULGARIA** every year to seek better lives in other countries. Many are willing initially to settle for jobs far below their level of education and training. **PRAY** that many of these young people will hear the gospel when they go abroad and will then return to their homeland to share the Good News.

Population: 7,538,000
Capital: Sofia
Language: Bulgarian
Literacy: 98%
Income (GDP) per capita: $6,600
Religions: Orthodox 70%, Muslim 11%,
    nonreligious 8%,
    various Christian 7%,
    Protestant 1%, Catholic 1%

Burkina Faso

The 12 million people of **BURKINA FASO** speak more than seventy different languages. As of 2001, the entire Bible was available in just six of those languages, and the New Testament in eleven. The Bible is, of course, available in French, the country's official language, but few people can read. **PRAY** for more and more missionaries who will learn these people's languages, so that the Burkinabe can at least *hear* the Gospel, and then someday read it as well.

Population: 12,228,000
Capital: Ouagadougou
Language: French
Literacy: 14%
Income (GDP) per capita: $1,100
Religions: Muslim 50%,
    traditional/indigenous 31%,
    Catholic 10%, Protestant 8%

Burundi

In the mountainous regions of **BURUNDI,** Christian workers walk many miles carrying generators on their heads in order to show the *Jesus* film in remote villages. Nine churches have been started as a result of this effort. **PRAY** that these new believers will have adequate training in the faith. Pray that many will go on to learn to read and that there will be enough Bibles for all of them.

Population: 6,096,000
Capital: Bujumbura
Language: Kirundi, French
Literacy: 19%
Income (GDP) per capita: $600
Religions: Catholic 57%, Protestant 13%,
    various Christian 10%, Anglican 8%,
    traditional/indigenous 7%, Muslim 3%

Cambodia

CAMBODIA has become a major destination for international prostitution rings that target young children. **PRAY** for the organizations that are trying, often at great personal risk, to rescue children from such circumstances. Pray that many of these children will instead find salvation in Christ and will find their way into a church family.

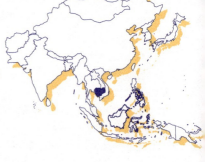

Population: 13,125,000
Capital: Phnom Penh
Language: Khmer, French
Literacy: 65%
Income (GDP) per capita: $1,500
Religions: Buddhist 82%,
   traditional/indigenous 9%,
   Muslim 4%, nonreligious 3%,
   various Christian 1%

Cameroon

Christianity has a long history in **CAMEROON,** but because of liberal theology and lack of discipleship, its churches are filled with nominal Christians, some of whom have low moral standards and mix pagan practices with their Christianity. **PRAY** that Cameroon would become a truly Christian nation.

Population: 15,746,000
Capital: Yaoundé
Language: French, English
Literacy: 63%
Income (GDP) per capita: $1,700
Religions: various Christian 28%,
   Catholic 26%, Muslim 25%,
   Protestant 14%, traditional/indigenous 5%

Canada

When United States Christians hear of the need for Bible translations, they may think of underdeveloped, tropical countries. But new or updated translations are needed in an estimated twenty-five languages in **CANADA,** mostly in remote northern areas. **PRAY** for young Christians with the love and commitment necessary for bringing God's written Word to these areas.

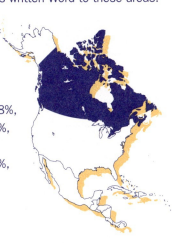

Population: 32,207,000
Capital: Ottawa
Language: English, French
Literacy: 99%
Income (GDP) per capita: $29,400
Religions: Catholic 40%, nonreligious 18%,
   various Christian 17%, Protestant 12%,
   Anglican 3%, Orthodox 2%,
   various Asian religions 2%, Muslim 2%,
   Jewish 1%, marginal Christian 1%

Chad

CHAD's literacy rate of 10 percent is one of the lowest in the world. Many of its people are nomads, living in harsh desert conditions with little opportunity for education or for communication with the outside world. **PRAY** for Christians with the love and vision to reach out to the people of Chad despite these obstacles.

Population: 9,253,000
Capital: N'Djamena
Language: French, Arabic
Literacy: 10%
Income (GDP) per capita: $1,100
Religions: Muslim 55%,
   traditional/indigenous 16%,
   Protestant 13%, various Christian 8%,
   Catholic 6%, Baha'i 1%

Chile

Though an estimated 15 percent of **CHILEANS** are evangelical Christians, their impact on society is often hindered by internal dissension. Estimates of the number of evangelical denominations range from one thousand to five thousand. **PRAY** for a nationwide revival that would bring these churches to a unity in faith and mission.

Population: 15,665,000
Capital: Santiago
Language: Spanish
Literacy: 95%
Income (GDP) per capita: $10,000
Religions: Catholic 70%,
    various Christian 15%, nonreligious 8%,
    marginal Christian 4%, Protestant 2%

People's Republic of China (mainland)

Average income has more than doubled in recent years in the **PEOPLE'S REPUBLIC OF CHINA.** But as many as 100 million Chinese have sunk into poverty as money-losing state-run businesses have been privatized, and workers have migrated to large cities in search of better lives. **PRAY** that the growing Christian churches of China will reach out to these displaced people.

Population: 1,286,975,000
Capital: Beijing
Language: Chinese
Literacy: 82%
Income (GDP) per capita: $4,400
Religions: nonreligious 50%,
    traditional/indigenous 31%,
    various Christian 8%, Buddhist 8%,
    Muslim 2%

Republic of China (Taiwan)

The government of **TAIWAN** recently announced that it wanted 3,000 Americans to teach in their schools in order to improve students' English-language skills. Taiwanese Christians are hoping that many of those positions will be filled by Christians. **PRAY** that this program will become an effective means of Gospel outreach.

Population: 22,603,000
Capital: Taipei
Language: Chinese
Literacy: 94%
Income (GDP) per capita: $18,000
Religions: traditional/indigenous 43%,
   Buddhist 25%, nonreligious 25%,
   various Christian 6%

Colombia

In **COLOMBIA,** notorious for its drug trafficking and civil warfare, a couple of groups of guerrilla soldiers have surrendered recently after having listened to Christian radio broadcasts for several years. **PRAY** for the worldwide outreach of Christian radio, which can reach individual hearts and minds in the seemingly most hopeless situations.

Population: 41,662,000
Capital: Bogotá
Language: Spanish
Literacy: 70%
Income (GDP) per capita: $6,500
Religions: Catholic 90%, Protestant 3%,
   various Christian 3%, nonreligious 3%

Republic of the Congo

Though virtually unknown in North America, malaria is a serious problem for lesser developed countries in tropical areas, such as the **REPUBLIC OF THE CONGO.** Worldwide, more than 3,000 children per day die of malaria. **PRAY** for those who live in areas where malaria is prevalent. Pray for the missionary medical personnel and others who seek to help them.

> Population: 2,954,000
> Capital: Brazzaville
> Language: French, Lingala
> Literacy: 63%
> Income (GDP) per capita: $900
> Religions: Catholic 50%,
>   various Christian 30%, Protestant 11%,
>   traditional/indigenous 5%,
>   nonreligious 2%, Muslim 1%

Democratic Republic of the Congo
(formerly Zaire)

The death toll in the years-long civil war in the **DEMOCRATIC REPUBLIC OF THE CONGO** has neared the 4 million mark. Though it is potentially Africa's richest nation, years of government corruption and competition over its wealth of natural resources has left it in shambles. **PRAY** for the Christians of Congo, who have remained strong amid the chaos, and have kept many of the schools and social agencies in operation.

> Population: 56,625,000
> Capital: Kinshasa
> Language: French, English
> Literacy: 77%
> Income (GDP) per capita: $610
> Religions: Catholic 42%,
>   various Christian 31%, Protestant 22%,
>   traditional/indigenous 3%, Muslim 1%

Cote d'Ivoire (Ivory Coast)

After many years of prosperity and political stability, **COTE D'IVOIRE** has seen civil strife in recent years, in part the result of tensions between Muslims and other religious and ethnic groups. **PRAY** that the nation's many well-established Christian missions will continue to be a center of stability and a light for the entire nation.

Population: 16,962,000
Capital: Yamoussoukro
Language: French
Literacy: 42%
Income (GDP) per capita: $1,500
Religions: Muslim 38%,
   traditional/indigenous 29%,
   Catholic 14%, Protestant 9%,
   various Christian 9%

Croatia

CROATIA is still recovering from many years of communist domination and then the regional ethnic strife of the post-communist era. Evangelical Christians are few in number. Yet an evangelical seminary begun in 1972, during communist days, has had a major impact throughout Europe. **PRAY** that this seminary will continue to be a beacon of truth in this nation and beyond.

Population: 4,422,000
Capital: Zagreb
Language: Croatian
Literacy: 97%
Income (GDP) per capita: $8,800
Religions: Catholic 87%,
   Orthodox 5%, Muslim 3%,
   nonreligious 2%, Protestant 1%

Cuba

Evangelical Christians in **CUBA** are offering marriage counseling services at several locations. Some estimate that Cuba's divorce rate is as high as 85 percent. **PRAY** that many marriages will be saved, and that many people will find new life in Christ through this ministry.

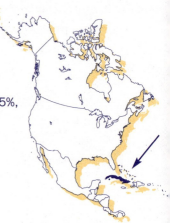

Population: 11,263,000
Capital: Havana
Language: Spanish
Literacy: 96%
Income (GDP) per capita: $2,300
Religions: Catholic 39%, nonreligious 35%,
    traditional/indigenous 17%,
    Protestant 3%, various Christian 3%,
    marginal Christian 2%

Denmark

For many years **DENMARK** has welcomed people from other nations as guest workers and refugees—as seen by the fact that 3 percent of the people in this far-northern nation are Muslim. But the international war on terrorism has brought tighter controls on immigration. **PRAY** that, despite understandable new fears, the Christians of Denmark would willingly share the Gospel with all who live among them.

Population: 5,384,000
Capital: Copenhagen
Language: Danish
Literacy: 99%
Income (GDP) per capita: $29,000
Religions: Protestant 78%,
    nonreligious 11%,
    various Christian 7%, Muslim 3%

Ecuador

With each government lasting an average of two years, **ECUADOR** desperately needs political stability and morally upright leaders. Meanwhile, there is a growing number of Christian ministries on the nation's college campuses. **PRAY** that the students reached by these ministries would go on to provide good leadership in all areas of society, from business to education to government.

Population: 13,710,000
Capital: Quito
Language: Spanish, Quechua
Literacy: 90%
Income (GDP) per capita: $3,200
Religions: Catholic 82%,
   various Christian 9%, Protestant 4%,
   marginal Christian 2%, nonreligious 2%

Egypt

Although **EGYPT** officially has freedom of religion, Muslims who convert to Christianity are often subject to imprisonment and torture. Government officials turn a blind eye while local police enforce Islamic law. **PRAY** that pressure from the Christian West will lead to better legal protection for Christians. Egypt receives billions of dollars annually in U.S. foreign aid.

Population: 74,719,000
Capital: Cairo
Language: Arabic
Literacy: 61%
Income (GDP) per capita: $3,900
Religions: Muslim 86%,
   Orthodox 12%, Protestant 1%

El Salvador

Some 70,000 people died in **EL SALVADOR's** civil war during the
1980s. Things have gotten better since then, and churches have grown
strong. Yet the war left a deep impact on society. An estimated 350,000
children were abandoned during the war. **PRAY** that many of those
children, who are now adults, will find salvation and a warm welcome in
evangelical churches.

> Population: 6,470,000
> Capital: San Salvador
> Language: Spanish
> Literacy: 74%
> Income (GDP) per capita: $4,700
> Religions: Catholic 70%,
>   Protestant 16%, various Christian 9%,
>   marginal Christian 2%, nonreligious 2%

Finland

Most people in **FINLAND** spend their whole lives as members of the
official state church, which is more evangelical than most state churches.
A comparatively high proportion of young Finns attend confirmation class.
PRAY that those classes would be a place where young people are truly
confronted with their need for a saving relationship with Jesus Christ.

> Population: 5,191,000
> Capital: Helsinki
> Language: Finnish, Swedish
> Literacy: 100%
> Income (GDP) per capita: $26,000
> Religions: Protestant 87%,
>   nonreligious 11%, Orthodox 1%

Prayer around the world Concerns

France

Though a majority of people in **FRANCE** claim to be Roman Catholic, the church's influence is declining. In 1970, 75 percent of children were baptized; today only 20 percent are. Meanwhile less than 1 percent of the population belong to evangelical churches. **PRAY** for revival throughout all the churches of France.

Population: 60,181,000
Capital: Paris
Language: French
Literacy: 99%
Income (GDP) per capita: $25,700
Religions: Catholic 68%,
    nonreligious 19%, Muslim 10%,
    Protestant 2%

Germany

Suicide is the second leading cause of death for people aged 15 to 29 in **GERMANY.** Worldwide, an estimated six people per day respond to requests for "suicide partners" in Internet chat rooms. **PRAY** for youth evangelists in Germany and around the world who seek to share the Gospel's message of real hope. Pray that people considering suicide will find instead the warmth and love of Christian fellowship.

Population: 82,398,000
Capital: Berlin
Language: German
Literacy: 100%
Income (GDP) per capita: $26,600
Religions: Protestant 34%,
    Catholic 33%, nonreligious 26%,
    Muslim 4%, Orthodox 1%,
    various Christian 1%

Guyana

The traditionally Christian nation of **GUYANA** has seen the rapid growth of both Hinduism and Islam through immigration. Thanks to rich nations like Saudi Arabia, it now has 130 mosques. **PRAY** that Christian churches and missions in Guyana will engage their culture with the truth of Jesus Christ.

Population: 702,000
Capital: Georgetown
Language: English, Amerindian dialects
Literacy: 98%
Income (GDP) per capita: $4,000
Religions: various Christian 44%,
 Hindu 33%, nonreligious 10%,
 Muslim 9%, indigenous 4%

Honduras

While many ministries have addressed the needs of the poor in **HONDURAS,** one missionary couple has targeted a neglected people group: middle- and upper-class people in the capital city. Their church is growing steadily, with many Hondurans taking active roles in its ministry. **PRAY** that this church will use its influence to bring economic prosperity and spiritual health to all of Honduras.

Population: 6,670,000
Capital: Tegucigalpa
Language: Spanish
Literacy: 73%
Income (GDP) per capita: $2,600
Religions: Catholic 79%, Protestant 13%,
 various Christian 4%,
 marginal Christian 2%,
 nonreligious 1%

Prayer Concerns around the world

Hungary

While Christians in the United States can choose from any number of Christian radio stations 24 hours a day, Christians in **HUNGARY** were able for the first time, in 2003, to hear evangelical broadcasting—for three hours per week! **PRAY** for the success and growth of this new Gospel outreach to this formerly communist nation.

Population: 10,045,000
Capital: Budapest
Language: Hungarian
Literacy: 99%
Income (GDP) per capita: $13,300
Religions: Catholic 60%,
   Protestant 21%,
   various Christian 10%,
   nonreligious 7%, Jewish 1%

India

Perhaps in response to the rapid growth of Christianity, **INDIA** has passed laws trying to limit conversions. One law, for instance, requires that a convert must have a secondary education—but one-third of India's people are illiterate. **PRAY** that the gospel will go forth despite such restrictions. Pray that many more Indians will learn to read and that one of their first books will be the Bible!

Population: 1,049,700,000
Capital: New Delhi
Language: Hindi, English
Literacy: 62%
Income (GDP) per capita: $2,500
Religions: Hindu 79%,
   Muslim 12%, Catholic 2%,
   Protestant 2%, Sikh 2%

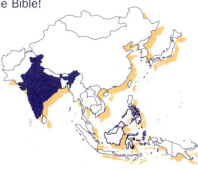

Indonesia

Though **INDONESIA** officially has freedom of religion, those who are not Muslim often face persecution. One province recently adopted Islamic law, and persecution has increased, with many Christians fleeing to other provinces. **PRAY** that Indonesian Christians will respond in godly ways to those who are enemies of the Gospel, and that many hearts will turn to Christ as a result.

> Population: 234,893,000
> Capital: Jakarta
> Language: Indonesian
> Literacy: 84%
> Income (GDP) per capita: $3,100
> Religions: Muslim 80%,
>   Protestant 7%, various Christian 5%,
>   Catholic 3%, Hindu 2%,
>   various Asian religions 2%

Iran

Most of the very few evangelical churches in **IRAN** were closed after the 1979 Islamic revolution. But the number of evangelicals has increased more than tenfold since then. Iranian Christians played a key role in relief efforts after the 2003 earthquake. **PRAY** that Iranian believers will remain faithful amid persecution and will continue to share Christ's love and His offer of eternal salvation.

> Population: 68,279,000
> Capital: Tehran
> Language: Farsi
> Literacy: 72%
> Income (GDP) per capita: $7,000
> Religions: Muslim 99%

Iraq

Even while **IRAQ** goes through times of crisis and change, many Christians from around the world are seeking to share Christ's love in this predominantly Muslim nation. **PRAY** that their efforts will build bridges of understanding and bring new hope to individual Iraqis, and that the Gospel will be heard in this ancient home of Abraham.

Population: 24,683,000
Capital: Baghdad
Language: Arabic
Literacy: 58%
Income (GDP) per capita: $2,400
Religions: Muslim 97%,
    Christian 2%

Ireland

IRELAND is a very young nation, with half of its people under the age of 28. Christian leaders are reaching out to these young people through campus ministries, street evangelism, and Christian camps. **PRAY** that these efforts will strengthen the church in Ireland and that it will remain a leader in world missions.

Population: 3,924,000
Capital: Dublin
Language: English, Irish Gaelic
Literacy: 99%
Income (GDP) per capita: $30,500
Religions: Catholic 87%,
    nonreligious 5%,
    various Christian 4%,
    Anglican 2%, Protestant 1%

Israel

An estimated 6,000 people—60 percent of them Jewish—meet in ninety Hebrew-speaking churches in **ISRAEL.** They are free to share their faith with anyone over age 18, and with those under 18 with parental permission. **PRAY** for the proclamation of the Gospel in this birthplace of Jesus Christ, where years of conflict have led many to search for truth.

Population: 6,117,000
Capital: Jerusalem
Language: Hebrew, Arabic
Literacy: 98%
Income (GDP) per capita: $19,000
Religions: Jewish 80%, Muslim 15%,
    Druze 2%, Catholic 1%

Italy

A literature distribution ministry in **ITALY** reports that they used to find many of their tracts discarded on the street, but now they find very few thrown away. One lady picked up a tract that *was* discarded—three weeks after it was handed out—and called in to accept its offer of salvation. **PRAY** that more and more of this ministry's tracts will be read and that many of those who read will respond.

Population: 57,998,000
Capital: Rome
Language: Italian
Literacy: 98%
Income (GDP) per capita: $25,000
Religions: Catholic 76%,
    nonreligious 20%, Muslim 2%,
    various Christian 1%

Jamaica

Although it advertises itself as a tropical paradise, **JAMAICA** has one of the world's highest homicide rates. This is true in part because, while Americans populate Jamaica's beaches, they also supply the market for its illegal drug trade. **PRAY** for the repentance and salvation of those involved with illegal drugs in Jamaica . . . and in the United States!

Population: 2,696,000
Capital: Kingston
Language: English, Creole
Literacy: 85%
Income (GDP) per capita: $3,900
Religions: Protestant 39%,
    various Christian 29%, Catholic 10%,
    Rastafarian 10%, nonreligious 5%,
    Anglican 4%, marginal Christian 1%

Japan

In **JAPAN,** workers are often transferred to new cities with little advance notice. Christian leaders are increasingly using this fact of life as an opportunity to start new home churches when Christians are transferred. **PRAY** for the success of such church-planting efforts in this nation where Christians are few and the average church has only twenty-seven members.

Population: 127,215,000
Capital: Tokyo
Language: Japanese
Literacy: 100%
Income (GDP) per capita: $28,000
Religions: Shinto or Buddhist 70%,
    new indigenous religions 24%,
    nonreligious 4%,
    various Christian 1%

Jordan

During the time between the two Gulf wars, more than fifty young Iraqi
Christians graduated from an evangelical Bible school in **JORDAN. PRAY**
that these young men will faithfully proclaim the Good News in Iraq. And
pray that the Bible school will be able to send more and more of its
graduates throughout the Middle East.

Population: 5,460,000
Capital: Amman
Language: Arabic
Literacy: 86%
Income (GDP) per capita: $4,300
Religions: Muslim 96%,
Orthodox 1%, Catholic 1%,
nonreligious 1%

Kazakhstan

The number of evangelical Christians in **KAZAKHSTAN** has grown
rapidly in the years since the nation abandoned communism. The new
government has tried to revive the Kazakh language, which was
deemphasized under communism. **PRAY** that a Christian radio ministry
that broadcasts into the nation will have the resources to increase the
amount of programming available in the Kazakh language.

Population: 16,764,000
Capital: Astana
Language: Kazakh, Russian
Literacy: 98%
Income (GDP) per capita: $6,300
Religions: Muslim 61%,
various Christian 16%,
nonreligious 14%, Orthodox 7%

Korea (North)

Because of its commitment to communism and long-term isolation from the rest of the world, **NORTH KOREA** has become very poor (compare its income per capita to that of democratic South Korea). There have been frequent famines, and whole families have been known to poison themselves rather than face slow death by starvation. **PRAY** that freedom, prosperity, and the Gospel will come soon to this suffering land.

Population: 22,466,000
Capital: Pyongyang
Language: Korean
Literacy: 99%
Income (GDP) per capita: $1,000
Religions: nonreligious 64%,
traditional/indigenous 16%,
Chondogyo 13%, Buddhist 4%,
various Christian 1%

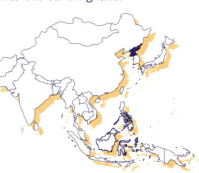

Korea (South)

As various nations have sought to address problems relating to the communist government of North Korea, the Christians of **SOUTH KOREA** have increased their efforts to reach out to North Koreans on a more personal level. They have provided food aid, and when North Koreans flee to other countries, they provide assistance such as job training. **PRAY** that these efforts will result in many finding salvation in Christ.

Population: 48,289,000
Capital: Seoul
Language: Korean
Literacy: 100%
Income (GDP) per capita: $19,400
Religions: Protestant 35%,
Buddhist 23%, nonreligious 15%,
various Asian religions 9%,
traditional/indigenous 8%, Catholic 7%,
marginal Christian 2%

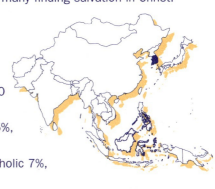

Laos

In **LAOS,** Christianity is considered the "enemy's religion" because it was introduced by foreign missionaries. Christians are urged to renounce their faith, and if they don't, they are often jailed. Despite such persecution, there is a growing demand for Bibles and Christian literature. **PRAY** that the Laotian church will continue to grow, with many more turning to Christ because of the bravery and faithfulness of these new believers.

Population: 5,922,000
Capital: Vientiane
Language: Lao, French
Literacy: 57%
Income (GDP) per capita: $1,700
Religions: Buddhist 61%,
    traditional/indigenous 31%,
    nonreligious 4%,
    various Christian 2%, Muslim 1%

Latvia

Christians in **LATVIA** and in several other nations formerly ruled by Soviet communism benefit from the ministry of an organization that promotes theological education in those countries. The group translates textbooks, trains teachers, and promotes high academic standards. **PRAY** for the continued success of this vital ministry in a part of the world where Christian education was forbidden for many decades.

Population: 2,349,000
Capital: Riga
Language: Latvian
Literacy: 100%
Income (GDP) per capita: $8,300
Religions: nonreligious 40%,
    Catholic 20%, Protestant 20%,
    various Christian 14%,
    Orthodox 4%

Prayer Concerns around the world

Liberia

During its long and bitter civil war, more than 15,000 children in **LIBERIA** were recruited to fight for all of the warring sides. **PRAY** for ongoing efforts to share the Gospel with them. Pray that as individuals respond to the Gospel, they will lead others to Christ and will help rebuild their nation.

Population: 3,317,000
Capital: Monrovia
Language: English
Literacy: 38%
Income (GDP) per capita: $1,100
Religions: traditional/indigenous 48%,
    various Christian 20%, Protestant 14%,
    Muslim 13%, Catholic 3%

Libya

In **LIBYA**—where almost everyone is Muslim, and Christianity is strictly forbidden—the only way to hear the Gospel is through the Internet or by radio or television broadcasts from outside the country. But who will follow up and disciple new believers? **PRAY** that the electronic media will, more and more, include resources for discipleship. Pray especially that Libya will soon have greater freedom of religion.

Population: 5,499,000
Capital: Tripoli
Language: Arabic, Italian
Literacy: 76%
Income (GDP) per capita: $7,600
Religions: Muslim 96%,
    Orthodox 1%, Catholic 1%

Macedonia

MACEDONIA is a nation composed of several ethnic groups which speak different languages, and there is often conflict between them. A Christian Cultural Center in the capital city includes a bookstore, but few Christian books are available in the Macedonian language. **PRAY** for translators who will commit themselves to meeting this need.

Population: 2,063,000
Capital: Skopje
Language: Macedonian, Albanian
Literacy: 89%
Income (GDP) per capita: $5,000
Religions: Orthodox 62%,
Muslim 25%, nonreligious 12%

Madagascar

Though there are many strong Christian churches in **MADAGASCAR,** many parts of the country remain unreached—in part because of the difficult terrain and lack of good roads. Meanwhile, Muslims are building mosques and schools throughout the nation. **PRAY** that the Holy Spirit would move in many hearts and that millions would come to salvation in Jesus Christ.

Population: 16,980,000
Capital: Antananarivo
Language: Malagasy, French
Literacy: 46%
Income (GDP) per capita: $760
Religions: traditional/indigenous 44%,
Protestant 27%, Catholic 20%,
Muslim 7%

Malawi

In 2003, Christians in **MALAWI** began receiving tens of thousands of copies of a new translation of the New Testament in their national Chichewa language. **PRAY** that this new translation will help make the Bible more understandable to the people of Malawi and surrounding nations. Chichewa is also a common language in Mozambique, Tanzania, Zambia, and Zimbabwe.

> Population: 11,651,000
> Capital: Lilongwe
> Language: English, Chichewa
> Literacy: 56%
> Income (GDP) per capita: $670
> Religions: Protestant 28%,
>   various Christian 26%, Catholic 23%,
>   Muslim 13%, traditional/indigenous 6%,
>   Anglican 2%

Mali

The West African nation of **MALI** has been a Muslim nation for seven centuries. But a military coup in 1991 led to greater democracy and religious freedom. Christian ministries are now welcomed. **PRAY** that the Christians of Mali, as well as missionaries from other nations, will respond to this day of opportunity for the Gospel in Mali.

> Population: 11,626,000
> Capital: Bamako
> Language: French
> Literacy: 31%
> Income (GDP) per capita: $860
> Religions: Muslim 87%,
>   traditional/indigenous 11%,
>   various Christian 2%

Mauritania

The harsh climate of **MAURITANIA,** with sandstorms more than half of the year, discourages people from the outside from living there. The religious climate of strict Islam forbids all missionary activity. Christian evangelism is punishable by death. **PRAY** for the very few Christians who work in secular jobs within the land, and pray for the evangelization of the thousands of Mauritanians who travel to or work in other nations.

Population: 2,913,000
Capital: Nouakchott
Language: Arabic, French
Literacy: 38%
Income (GDP) per capita: $2,000
Religions: Muslim 99%

Mexico

Forty percent of the residents of Chiapas, the southernmost state in **MEXICO**, are evangelical Christians. Recently, however, some 300 evangelical Christian families from that state were converted to Islam by Muslim missionaries from Spain. **PRAY** that Christians everywhere would be vigilant in their proclamation and defense of the Gospel, and in the discipleship of believers.

Population: 104,908,000
Capital: Mexico City
Language: Spanish
Literacy: 89%
Income (GDP) per capita: $9,000
Religions: Catholic 88%,
    Protestant 6%, nonreligious 4%

Morocco

Tens of thousands of **MOROCCANS** have emigrated to Europe in search of work; more than 3,000 have drowned trying to cross the Straits of Gibraltar illegally. **PRAY** for the many ongoing efforts to evangelize Moroccans living in Europe. Christian evangelism is illegal in Morocco, and less than a thousand Moroccan nationals are known to have become Christians.

Population: 31,689,000
Capital: Rabat
Language: Arabic, French
Literacy: 44%
Income (GDP) per capita: $3,900
Religions: Muslim 99%

New Zealand

NEW ZEALAND has many strong evangelical churches, but there are many people who consider themselves "nonreligious." Some of the strongest church growth has been among Korean immigrants, who have started dozens of new churches. **PRAY** for harmony between the Korean and the native New Zealander churches, as they both reach out to the culture around them.

Population: 3,951,000
Capital: Wellington
Language: English, Maori
Literacy: 99%
Income (GDP) per capita: $20,200
Religions: nonreligious 35%,
   Protestant 20%, Anglican 15%,
   Catholic 12%, various Christian 9%,
   marginal Christian 4%,
   various Asian religions 3%

Niger

NIGER needs literacy training, and it needs God's written Word.
More than a dozen of the nation's tribal languages have no Scripture.
Worldwide, more than 3,000 languages still have no Scripture. **PRAY**
for men and women who are willing to commit a major part of their
vocational life to concentrate on bringing the Bible to just one
language group.

> Population: 11,059,000
> Capital: Niamey
> Language: French, Hausa
> Literacy: 17%
> Income (GDP) per capita: $830
> Religions: Muslim 97%,
>   traditional/indigenous 2%

Nigeria

Funded in part by oil-rich middle Eastern nations, Islam continues to
grow in **NIGERIA.** But Christian churches are also growing. In 2003, a
new Christian university was established on 500 acres of land near the
capital city. **PRAY** that it will become a vibrant center for evangelism
and for educating strong leaders for churches throughout Nigeria and all
of Africa.

> Population: 133,882,000
> Capital: Abuja
> Language: English, Hausa
> Literacy: 64%
> Income (GDP) per capita: $875
> Religions: Muslim 41%,
>   various Christian 18%, Catholic 12%,
>   Protestant 12%, Anglican 10%,
>   traditional/indigenous 6%

around the world
Prayer Concerns

Oman

Though most in **OMAN** are Muslim, Christian missionaries have lived there since 1890, and mission hospitals have become part of the government healthcare system. Many foreign Christians work in various other secular jobs, and are welcome to stay—as long as they don't try to convert Muslims. **PRAY** that these Christians would live exemplary lives among their Muslim friends and coworkers.

Population: 2,807,000
Capital: Muscat
Language: Arabic
Literacy: 67%
Income (GDP) per capita: $8,300
Religions: Muslim 92%, Hindu 3%,
   various Christian 2%, Buddhist 1%

Pakistan

Several Christians in **PAKISTAN** have been arrested in recent years on charges of blasphemy against Mohammed. The mandatory penalty is death, though sometimes this is reduced to a life sentence. **PRAY** that the fear of breaking such laws will not cause Christians to waver in their commitment to Jesus Christ as the only name "by which we must be saved" (Acts 4:12).

Population: 150,695,000
Capital: Islamabad
Language: Urdu, English
Literacy: 38%
Income (GDP) per capita: $2,100
Religions: Muslim 96%,
   various Christian 2%, Hindu 1%

161

Panama

PANAMA is prosperous, largely because of the Panama Canal. And its churches have grown rapidly. Yet the country's 72 percent illegitimacy rate shows that not all is well. **PRAY** for true revival throughout all the churches of Panama. With the widespread illegitimacy comes many fatherless families, so pray for stronger leadership in both families and churches.

Population: 2,961,000
Capital: Panama City
Language: Spanish
Literacy: 91%
Income (GDP) per capita: $6,000
Religions: Catholic 71%, Protestant 14%,
    various Christian 3%, Muslim 3%,
    nonreligious 3%, Buddhist 2%,
    Baha'i 1%, Sikh 1%,
    marginal Christian 1%

Paraguay

PARAGUAY is divided between the vast majority who are of mixed Spanish and Guaraní descent and are primarily Catholic, and the minority of European descent who are mainly Protestant. **PRAY** that there would be increased communication between these two groups, as they share their strengths in reaching those who still need to hear the gospel.

Population: 6,037,000
Capital: Asunción
Language: Spanish, Guaraní
Literacy: 90%
Income (GDP) per capita: $4,200
Religions: Catholic 85%, various Christian 7%,
    Protestant 5%, nonreligious 1%

Peru

Bible-believing churches have grown rapidly in **PERU** in spite of—or perhaps because of—widespread civil warfare and extreme poverty. Yet there are still large areas of the country where the gospel is not being proclaimed. **PRAY** that the Christians of Peru will increasingly have a vision for reaching their own nation.

Population: 28,410,000
Capital: Lima
Language: Spanish, Quechua
Literacy: 87%
Income (GDP) per capita: $4,800
Religions: Catholic 65%,
   various Christian 16%, nonreligious 8%,
   Protestant 6%, marginal Christian 3%,
   traditional/indigenous 1%

Poland

The formerly communist nation of **POLAND** is the scene of vibrant Christian activity. Almost all of the universities have Christian ministries on campus, and many Christian books are being translated into Polish and sold in bookstores. **PRAY** that the message of the gospel would be proclaimed more and more in this nation that suffered so much in the past century for its Christian faith.

Population: 38,623,000
Capital: Warsaw
Language: Polish
Literacy: 99%
Income (GDP) per capita: $9,500
Religions: Catholic 78%,
   various Christian 10%,
   nonreligious 10%, Orthodox 1%

Russia

With the collapse of Soviet communism came also the collapse of **RUSSIA'S** social welfare system. Today, one-tenth of its children are homeless. Russian churches, which had been excluded from welfare work under communism, are just now beginning to address the problem. **PRAY** that these churches will learn how to meet the needs of these young people, and that many of them will find eternal salvation.

Population: 144,526,000
Capital: Moscow
Language: Russian
Literacy: 98%
Income (GDP) per capita: $9,300
Religions: Orthodox 41%,
    nonreligious 31%,
    various Christian 11%,
    Muslim 10%, various other religions 4%, Catholic 1%

Senegal

There are few evangelical Christians in **SENEGAL,** and they are scattered among the mostly Muslim population. Christians face constant pressure from relatives to convert to Islam. And young Christians are often tempted to marry Muslims because there are so few potential spouses to choose among within the churches. **PRAY** for strength for all who face such daily challenges to their faith.

Population: 10,580,000
Capital: Dakar
Language: French, Wolof
Literacy: 33%
Income (GDP) per capita: $1,500
Religions: Muslim 92%, Catholic 4%,
    traditional/indigenous 3%

Singapore

The church is growing in **SINGAPORE,** with an estimated one-third of all current college students claiming to be Christians. But as students grow older and take their place in the nation's booming economy, they often grow less fervent in their faith and their church involvement. **PRAY** for an ongoing revival among the churches of Singapore, which are crucial to evangelizing non-Christian Asia.

Population: 4,609,000
Capital: Singapore
Language: Chinese, Malay
Literacy: 90%
Income (GDP) per capita: $24,000
Religions: Buddhist 42%,
   Muslim 15%, nonreligious 15%,
   traditional Chinese religions 9%,
   Protestant 5%, Catholic 4%, Hindu 4%,
   various Christian 4%

Slovakia

SLOVAKIA has been a nominally Christian nation for many centuries, but revival is needed throughout all of its churches. There are some 6,000 towns and villages that do not have a strong Bible-teaching church. **PRAY** for Christian leaders with a vision to plant new churches. Pray for missionaries who will choose Slovakia as their place of ministry.

Population: 5,430,000
Capital: Bratislava
Language: Slovak
Literacy: 96%
Income (GDP) per capita: $12,200
Religions: Catholic 62%,
   nonreligious 17%,
   various Christian 11%,
   Protestant 9%

Slovenia

The Christians of **SLOVENIA** now have a new translation of the Bible in their own language. And even though, as of 2001, there was only one evangelical Christian bookstore in the nation, Christian literature has been distributed to most of the nation's homes. **PRAY** that such efforts will bear fruit. Pray especially that many Slovenians will receive these new Bibles.

> Population: 1,936,000
> Capital: Ljubljana
> Language: Slovenian, Serbo-Croatian
> Literacy: 99%
> Income (GDP) per capita: $18,000
> Religions: Catholic 81%,
>   nonreligious 13%, Orthodox 2%,
>   Muslim 1%, Protestant 1%

Somalia

SOMALIA has the dubious distinction of being considered the world's most lawless nation. In recent years as many as four different governments have ruled various areas simultaneously. Radical Muslims have offered Islamic law as the answer. Meanwhile, Somali Bibles have been distributed in certain areas despite government restrictions. **PRAY** that God's Word will bring peace and salvation to Somalia.

> Population: 8,025,000
> Capital: Mogadishu
> Language: Somali, Arabic
> Literacy: 24%
> Income (GDP) per capita: $550
> Religions: Muslim 99%

South Africa

Christians in **SOUTH AFRICA** have sponsored several "days of prayer and repentance" in recent years, with believers filling as many as seventy-five stadiums in one day for the events. **PRAY** that these gatherings will help heal forever the wounds of racial strife, and will bring revival to churches and a new vision for taking the gospel throughout southern Africa.

Population: 42,769,000
Capital: Pretoria
Language: English, Afrikaans
Literacy: 82%
Income (GDP) per capita: $10,000
Religions: various Christian 40%,
    Protestant 21%, traditional/indigenous 15%,
    Catholic 8%, nonreligious 8%,
    Anglican 4%, Muslim 1%, Hindu 1%

Spain

Statistics show the need for the gospel in **SPAIN.** In 1975, 61 percent of Spaniards said they attended church regularly. Today, just 19 percent do so. **PRAY** for revival throughout all the churches of Spain—the Catholic churches to which a majority of Spaniards officially belong, as well as the Protestant churches, many of which have been started by Christians from other nations.

Population: 40,217,000
Capital: Madrid
Language: Spanish
Literacy: 97%
Income per capita: $20,700
Religions: Catholic 66%,
    nonreligious 30%, Protestant 1%,
    various Christian 1%, Muslim 1%

Sudan

In **SUDAN,** the Muslim-led government has long required all its citizens to learn Arabic and to read the Qur'an in school. But these policies have actually helped spread the gospel, as Christians have become familiar with Islam and have been able to witness to Muslims. **PRAY** that the gospel will continue to prosper. Pray also for the many Sudanese Christians who are persecuted for their faith.

Population: 38,114,000
Capital: Khartoum
Language: Arabic, English
Literacy: 40%
Income (GDP) per capita: $1,400
Religions: Muslim 65%, Catholic 12%,
    traditional/indigenous 10%, Anglican 7%,
    Protestant 3%, nonreligious 1%

Sweden

Despite its far-northern location, **SWEDEN** is a prosperous nation and a key part of the world economy. An international department store chain based in Sweden boasts that it prints more catalogs worldwide than the number of Bibles being printed. **PRAY** that Swedes, and anyone else who receives that catalog, would find the Bible more interesting!

Population: 8,878,000
Capital: Stockholm
Language: Swedish
Literacy: 99%
Income (GDP) per capita: $25,400
Religions: Protestant 54%,
    nonreligious 40%, Muslim 3%,
    Catholic 1%, Orthodox 1%

Switzerland

SWITZERLAND, long isolated from the outside world by its high mountains, is becoming more and more internationalized as people come there for employment. One-third of the people in Geneva are non-Swiss. Many churches are evangelizing these new arrivals. **PRAY** that these vital ministries will bring many into God's kingdom, and that the Gospel will spread from Switzerland to the homelands of these immigrants.

Population: 7,319,000
Capital: Bern
Language: German, French
Literacy: 99%
Income (GDP) per capita: $31,700
Religions: Catholic 44%,
   Protestant 40%,
   nonreligious 8%, Muslim 3%,
   various other religions 2%,
   Orthodox 1%, various Christian 1%

Tanzania

TANZANIA came into being as a nation in the 1960s through a union of Tanganyika and the island of Zanzibar. Its people speak 135 different languages, only seventeen of which have Bible translations. **PRAY** for a new generation of Bible translators to address the unfinished task in nations such as Tanzania.

Population: 35,922,000
Capital: Dar es Salaam
Language: Swahili, English
Literacy: 68%
Income (GDP) per capita: $630
Religions: Muslim 32%, Catholic 24%,
   Protestant 17%, traditional/indigenous 15%,
   Anglican 8%, various Christian 3%

Prayer Concerns

Turkey

Though 99 percent of the people of **TURKEY** are Muslim, more and more of them are celebrating Christmas. They are attracted by Santa Claus and the gift giving and are largely unaware of the holiday's religious significance. **PRAY** that many in Turkey would somehow, through their annual celebration, discover the true meaning of Christmas.

Population: 68,109,000
Capital: Ankara
Language: Turkish
Literacy: 82%
Income (GDP) per capita: $7,000
Religions: Muslim 99%

Turkmenistan

The formerly communist nation of **TURKMENISTAN** is struggling economically, and its educational system is in crisis. Meanwhile, several brand-new schools, with brand-new computers, have been built—by militant Muslims. **PRAY** that the students selected to attend these schools will discover God's truth and will be set free.

Population: 4,776,000
Capital: Ashgabat
Language: Turkmen
Literacy: 98%
Income (GDP) per capita: $5,500
Religions: Muslim 92%,
    nonreligious 5%, Orthodox 2%

Uganda

As **UGANDA** continues its slow but steady recovery from the years of Idi Amin, revival has spread throughout its churches, from Catholic to evangelical, as nationals and Christians from other nations work together to rebuild the nation and meet its many pressing needs. **PRAY** that the revival will continue, and that many more will find eternal salvation.

Population: 25,633,000
Capital: Kampala
Language: English, Swahili
Literacy: 62%
Income (GDP) per capita: $1,300
Religions: Catholic 42%,
  Anglican 40%, Protestant 6%,
  Muslim 6%, traditional/indigenous 4%

United Arab Emirates

The **UNITED ARAB EMIRATES** has used its oil wealth to turn their nation into a favorite destination of tourists and shoppers from the Middle East and beyond. This has meant the importation of many foreign workers—and their non-Muslim religions. **PRAY** that increasing contact with the outside world will make Muslims in this nation more open to the Gospel.

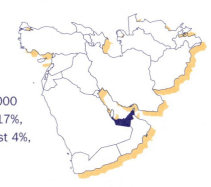

Population: 2,485,000
Capital: Abu Dhabi
Language: Arabic
Literacy: 79%
Income (GDP) per capita: $22,000
Religions: Muslim 65%, Hindu 17%,
  various Christian 9%, Buddhist 4%,
  various other religions 2%,
  nonreligious 1%

United Kingdom

Many in the West were shocked in April 2003 to learn that two suicide bombers in Israel had been recruited from the streets of London. One Christian ministry in London continually confronts radical Muslims during public debates in Hyde Park. **PRAY** that many more Christians in England will wake up to this very urgent mission field right on their doorstep.

Population: 60,095,000
Capital: London
Language: English
Literacy: 98%
Income (GDP) per capita: $25,300
Religions: Anglican 43%, nonreligious 28%,
   Catholic 10%, Protestant 7%,
   various Christian 4%, Muslim 2%,
   various Asian religions 2%,
   marginal Christian 2%

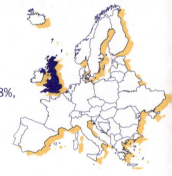

United States

A recent survey found that the **UNITED STATES OF AMERICA** is by far the most "religious" of the world's wealthy nations. While 59 percent of Americans said that religion is very important to them, only a third of British and just 11 percent of French respondents made that claim. **PRAY** that more and more Americans would place their faith in Jesus Christ and that their faith would be much more than just an answer on a survey.

Population: 290,343,000
Capital: Washington, D.C.
Language: English
Literacy: 96%
Income (GDP) per capita: $37,600
Religions: various Christian 38%,
   Protestant 24%, Catholic 21%,
   nonreligious 9%, Jewish 2%,
   Orthodox 2%, various Asian and
   other religions 2%, Muslim 1%

Uruguay

Our statistics for **URUGUAY** say that 49 percent are Catholic and 25 percent are nonreligious. But the fact that only about 1 percent of Catholics attend mass regularly suggests that most of them belong in the nonreligious category as well. **PRAY** for revival in this prosperous and very secularized nation.

Population: 3,413,000
Capital: Montevideo
Language: Spanish
Literacy: 98%
Income (GDP) per capita: $7,800
Religions: Catholic 49%, nonreligious 25%,
   traditional/indigenous 12%, Protestant 3%,
   various Christian 3%, marginal Christian 3%,
   Jewish 2%, Orthodox 1%

Uzbekistan

Since **UZBEKISTAN** became free from Soviet domination in 1991, Muslims funded by oil-rich nations have built more than 6,000 mosques. Christians, meanwhile, are persecuted. They are told they can have privileges by registering with the government, but then their applications are discarded. **PRAY** that Christians will courageously bear witness to their faith despite this persecution.

Population: 25,982,000
Capital: Tashkent
Language: Uzbek, Russian
Literacy: 97%
Income (GDP) per capita: $2,500
Religions: Muslim 83%,
   nonreligious 14%,
   various Christian 1%

Prayer Concerns around the world

Venezuela

Evangelical churches in **VENEZUELA** are accepting the challenge of the Great Commission, with missionaries serving in two dozen other nations and among various Amerindian people groups in Venezuela. These internal missions are often opposed by liberal anthropologists, who feel that tribal cultures should not be disturbed. **PRAY** that Venezuelan Christians will keep on proclaiming Jesus Christ, who gave His life "for the sins of the whole world" (1 John 2:2).

> Population: 24,655,000
> Capital: Caracas
> Language: Spanish
> Literacy: 91%
> Income (GDP) per capita: $5,500
> Religions: Catholic 89%, various Christian 5%,
>   Protestant 4%, nonreligious 1%

Zambia

Huge percentages of the population of **ZAMBIA** and other nations in southern Africa suffer from AIDS and from various tropical illnesses with symptoms similar to AIDS. Accurate diagnoses are not always possible due to the lack of medical technology. **PRAY** for the church in Zambia to reach out in compassion to those who suffer from AIDS and that many will turn to Jesus and find eternal salvation.

> Population: 10,307,000
> Capital: Lusaka
> Language: English
> Literacy: 78%
> Income (GDP) per capita: $890
> Religions: Protestant 34%, Catholic 32%,
>   various Christian 17%,
>   traditional/indigenous 12%,
>   marginal Christian 4%, Muslim 1%

Remember these other nations . . .

The worldwide family of nations is nearly two hundred-strong. Space allows the inclusion of only about half of those nations in this volume. The following were not included, but deserve a place in our prayers.

Andorra
Antigua/Barbuda
Armenia
Austria
Bahamas
Bahrain
Bangladesh
Barbados
Belgium
Belize
Benin
Bhutan
Bolivia
Bosnia and
  Herzegovina
Botswana
Brunei Darussalam
Cape Verde
Central African
  Republic
Comoros
Costa Rica
Cyprus
Czech Republic
Djibouti
Dominica
Dominican Republic
East Timor
Equatorial Guinea
Eritrea
Estonia
Ethiopia
Fiji
Gabon
Gambia
Georgia

Ghana
Greece
Grenada
Guatemala
Guinea
Guinea-Bissau
Haiti
Iceland
Kenya
Kiribati
Kuwait
Kyrgyzstan
Lebanon
Lesotho
Liechtenstein
Lithuania
Luxembourg
Malaysia
Maldives
Malta
Marshall Islands
Mauritius
Micronesia
Moldova
Monaco
Mongolia
Mozambique
Myanmar
  (formerly Burma)
Namibia
Nauru
Nepal
Netherlands
Nicaragua
Norway
Palau

Papua New Guinea
Philippines
Portugal
Qatar
Romania
Rwanda
Samoa
San Marino
Sao Tome/Principe
Saudi Arabia
Serbia and
  Montenegro
Seychelles
Sierra Leone
Solomon Islands
Sri Lanka
St. Kitts/Nevis
St. Lucia
St.Vincent/Grenadines
Suriname
Swaziland
Syria
Tajikistan
Thailand
Togo
Tonga
Trinidad/Tobago
Tunisia
Tuvalu
Ukraine
Vanuatu
Vatican City State
Vietnam
Western Sahara
Yemen
Zimbabwe

Sources

Christianity Today magazine.

The Church Around the World newsletter (Carol Stream, Ill.: Tyndale).

Mary Katherine Compton and David Compton, *Forbidden Fruit Creates Many Jams* (New York: New American Library, 2001).

Famous Quotations Network (famous-quotations.com).

Patrick Johnstone and Jason Mandryk, *Operation World* (Minneapolis: Bethany, 2001).

Pulse newsletter (published by Evangelism and Missions Information Service of the Billy Graham Center at Wheaton College, P.O. Box 794, Wheaton, IL 60189).

QuoteArchive.com.

Quotable Quotes (Pleasantville, N.Y.: The Reader's Digest Association, 1997).

QuoteWorld.org.

Thirty Days Muslim Prayer Focus (2001), distributed by WorldChristian News and Books, Colorado Springs, Colorado.

U.S. News and World Report.

Mark Water, compiler, *The New Encyclopedia of Christian Quotations* (Grand Rapids, Mich.: Baker, 2000).

World magazine.

John W. Wright, ed., *The New York Times 2004 Almanac* (New York: Penguin, 2003).